FOLK RELIGION IN AN URBAN SETTING

a Study of Hakka Villagers in Transition

Morris I. Berkowitz
Chung Chi College, Chinese University of Hong Kong
and University of Pittsburgh

Frederick P. Brandauer
Christian Study Centre on Chinese Religion and Culture

John H. Reed
American Baptist Mission

Hong Kong
Christian Study Centre on Chinese Religion and Culture
Tao Fong Shan, New Territories

Library of Congress Catalog Card Number: 71–86967

Printed by
Empire Printing Co., Tung Chong Factory Bldg., 653, King's Road, 2nd fl., Hong Kong.

The Christian Study Centre on Chinese Religion and Culture is engaged in scientific research with the aim of assisting the church in its total task of witness and service through increased understanding of the cultures in which it is situated.

To our wives :

Janice

Mildred

Kathleen

FOREWORD

Publication of this report is sponsored by the Christian Study Centre on Chinese Religion and Culture. The need for a survey on religious beliefs in Hong Kong with its society remoulded by a process of rapid social change will hardly be questioned within the Christian churches nor by those who take an active interest in human life in Hong Kong. The Plover Cove Resettlement may not be representative for life in Hong Kong on the whole, but it offered itself to the Christian Study Centre for very practical reasons.

The survey presented here is only a first step towards an investigation into religious beliefs. It is to be hoped that further substantiation will follow.

The Christian Study Centre expresses its thanks and appreciation to the three authors, Dr. M. I. Berkowitz, Rev. F. P. Brandauer, and Mr. J. H. Reed for their cooperation and for the services rendered in the writing of this report.

The survey is published simultaneously in *Ching Feng, Quarterly Notes on Christianity and Chinese Religion and Culture,* Vol. XII, No. 3 and 4 (1969).

Winfried Glüer
Tao Fong Shan, Shatin, N.T.
Hong Kong, September 1969

PREFACE

This study was planned as a first step in a projected study programme to gain an understanding of the total religious situation in Hong Kong. Prior to its inception, several individuals associated with the Christian Study Centre on Chinese Religion and Culture had suggested that the Centre undertake a field study of Chinese religion. Although literature describing classical Chinese religion is voluminous, these persons agreed that the forces of urbanization and secularization and the discontinuity with the past experienced by many Hong Kong people would make a new study invaluable. In addition, there were those who wanted to study the relation of Western religions to the total religious milieu of Hong Kong, particularly assessing not only the impact of Christianity, but also the extent of influence of traditional Chinese religion on Christian Chinese.

Accordingly, in early 1968, the staff of the Christian Study Centre called together a group of interested persons and professional consultants. After two or three meetings in which the authors of the present study took part, there emerged some rather broad purposes of a proposed extended study programme to be conducted by the Centre. One of these purposes was to determine the nature and extent of religious practices in Hong Kong; a second purpose was to understand the meaning of these practices for the people.

Because of the limited resources available to the Study Centre, the most expedient method of approaching the study of religious practices was to join with other individuals or groups doing or planning similar research. This approach would allow work in different locales (i.e., resettlement estates, low cost housing, squatter areas, etc.) with minimum expense in gathering basic descriptive data. Further, it was decided that an approach relying heavily on observation and utilizing some depth interviews would yield better results than a survey.[1]

A group of villagers had been relocated from a rural area called Plover Cove to the market town of Tai Po. Berkowitz had already

---

[1] A description and discussion of methodological considerations is to be found in the section entitled, "Notes on Methodology."

begun research on these villagers and offered to this project data collected for his study as well as the use of an apartment which had been rented in the blocks in which the villagers live.[2] Discussion of this possibility resolved certain administrative and financial issues and resulted in the decision that the project should proceed on a cooperative basis. This decision was based partly on financial grounds (starting a new project somewhere else would have been far more expensive), partly on practical grounds (a pooling of the technical skills of three workers seemed more promising than a smaller work group), partly on the grounds of the availability of a great deal of background data (all Government records concerning this group had been searched as well as interview information gathered and processed), and finally on principle (we saw no reason why many small research projects should be attempted when cooperation would be much more likely to produce more interesting and satisfying research).

In summary, the present study is the first in what we hope will be a series of sociological studies of religion in various locations in Hong Kong. The two objectives of this study are to describe the religious practices as they were observed in the resettlement area and to interpret and analyze the meaning of the practices where it is possible and desirable.

A major problem was to determine who the readers of this volume might be. The authors realized that readers could be laymen unfamiliar with the language and literature of the social sciences. At the same time a work of this nature could attract the interest of sinologists, scholars of religion, sociologists and anthropologists. A further group of readers might come from those interested in Hong Kong and Hong Kong life. Most of the decisions with regard to style were made with these considerations in mind. Much of the scholarly material is to be found in the footnotes. Some readers may wish to disregard them, although there are some footnotes which add

---

2 This particular study is an adjunct to a larger study of these resettled villagers in which Dr. Berkowitz is collaborating with Mr. Eddie K. K. Poon. The other study deals with social change as a result of the removal of the villagers to an urban area. The report of that study, which will contain a chapter on religion, will most likely be published in 1970 under the tentative title, *Peasant to Landlord: A Study of Social Change.* A preliminary report of this study is contained in Morris I. Berkowitz, "Plover Cove Village to Tai Po Market: A Study in Forced Migration," *Journal of the Hong Kong Branch of the Royal Asiatic Society,* VIII (August, 1968), pp. 96-108.

explanation and information to the text which make it more meaningful and interesting. Chapter I is basically theoretical and therefore may be of less interest to the lay reader than later chapters; he may wish to postpone reading this chapter until he has finished the rest of the volume. Since this volume is being published in Hong Kong we have chosen to use *The Oxford Dictionary* as the standard for spelling.

The translation and rendering of Chinese place names, proper nouns and certain concepts posed some rather knotty problems. In most cases romanized Chinese has been used. Where concepts were involved we have indicated the meaning or near meaning in parentheses or in a footnote. Without entering into a discussion of the relative merits of different romanization systems, the authors have chosen to use the Pinyin Latinization because it is the romanization system officially recognized by China, it is becoming more and more widely used by scholars, and it is as adequate as any other system. Nomenclature follows the accepted Chinese practice. Since with few exceptions the romanizations are for single terms, we have not followed the convention of grouping character combinations. For the serious scholar we have included the character(s) usually after the first usage of each term as well as a glossary containing the romanizations and the characters. For place names and certain other proper nouns we have used the officially recognized romanization to be found in the Government Gazetteer.[3] For the convenience of Cantonese speaking readers the Yale Cantonese romanizations have been included in the glossary.[4]

As social scientists we are concerned with reporting as accurately, objectively and respectfully as possible. To this end we have adopted the convention of capitalizing the names of deities to which we make reference as we would capitalize references to the deity in the West.

When this volume was written the approximate rate of exchange between the Hong Kong dollar and the American dollar was six : one and the Hong Kong dollar to the British pound fourteen : one. All reference to currency in this volume is in Hong Kong dollars.

---

3 *A Gazetteer of Place Names in Hong Kong, Kowloon and the New Territories* (Hong Kong: Hong Kong Government Press, 1960).

4 Parker P. F. Huang, *Speak Cantonese, Books I-III* (New Haven: Far Eastern Publications, Yale University, 1962).

Finally, the authors want to thank all of those persons who have contributed to this research. We are most indebted to Mr. C. Jong, Miss Pang Ken Phin and Mr. Thu En Yu who spent a summer as observers in the Tai Po Resettlement Area. We are equally indebted to Mr. James Ma and Miss Fok Man Ching who provided translation skills to the project. We would also like to acknowledge the assistance of Mr. Eddie K. K. Poon and Miss Deborah Strong Davis, tutors at Chung Chi College, and Miss Catherine C. Swatek as well as many other students of Dr. Berkowitz, all of whom were involved in gathering data and in locating documentation and theoretical materials. The very excellent drawing of a village house is the work of Mr. Wu Chie Hong. We appreciate very much the cooperation and contributions of Dr. Dorothy Heid Bracey who gave advice and counsel to the observers and who provided us with data gathered on some of the villagers prior to removal. Dr. Marjorie J. Topley provided helpful guidance in the planning stage of this project.

The representatives of the Hong Kong Government with whom we dealt were unfailingly interested and cooperative. The Government Information Service kindly provided the photograph for the cover of the book.

Research reports are made out of the tedium of filing, typing, cutting and pasting: Kathie Reed bore the major burden of this work and was ably assisted by Janice Berkowitz, Alice Yu, Diane Nitchman, Tam Wai Hang and Marion Kwan. Dr. Andrew T. Roy read the manuscript, and drawing upon his many years of study and knowledge of Chinese culture and religion provided invaluable suggestions and corrections.

Our very special thanks go to Mrs. William D. Hackett who unstintingly gave of her time and editorial skills to make this volume more readable.

Although many people have been involved in the preparation of this volume the authors take the ultimate responsibility for its contents and form.

The Plover Cove villagers let us look at their lives. Their willingness to share, their graciousness to our observers and the dignity of their way of life have contributed more to us than these simple words can indicate.

M. I. B.
F. P. B.
J. H. R.
September, 1969

CONTENTS

CHAPTER I

PERSPECTIVES ON FOLK RELIGION

The social scientific study of religion attempts to take what has been called a "naturalistic approach to religion."[1] That is, the sociologist is concerned with the reasons both for the existence of religion and for the resulting phenomena in human behaviour. He seeks to understand behaviour in terms of natural causes and effects, or to put it another way, he seeks to answer the question: what part does religion play in society? Unlike the religionist who may be interested in proving religious truths, the sociologist is concerned with understanding that behaviour which is classified as religious. Goode has pointed out that sociological analysis of religion is not to be used for determining the origin of religion, for making a determination of which religion is the right one or for determining the goodness or badness of religion.[2] What we are attempting in this study is an objective description and analysis of an aspect of human behaviour rather than a subjective judgement about the truth claims of a particular religion. In using this naturalistic approach we will be relying heavily on the theoretical framework of structural-functionalism.

From the functional viewpoint, the sociologist sees society as an integrated whole made up of structurally related elements, each of which has one or more functions.[3] For example, religion can be seen as one of many structurally related elements, usually called "institutions," in a society. The word "institution" refers to patterned behaviour of people within the society which is usually directed toward one sphere of social activity. For example, all a society's patterns of behaviour which are directed toward supplying basic goods and services to that society are collectively called the "institution of economics" within the society. But these patterns of behaviour are not unrelated

---

1 Thomas F. O'Dea, *The Sociology of Religion* (Englewood Cliffs, New Jersey: Prentice-Hall, 1966), pp. 17-18.

2 William J. Goode, *Religion Among the Primitives* (Glencoe, Illinois: The Free Press, 1951), pp. 22-23.

3 Robert K. Merton, *Social Theory and Social Structure* (New York: The Free Press, 1957), pp. 19-84.

to one another, and behavioural patterns which are nominally economic may also have religious implications, governmental implications and so forth.   Similarly, not all institutions can coexist with all other possible social arrangements: there must be some meshing and consistency in the arrangement of institutions within any society.   Religious and economic institutions support one another, and some authors have postulated a "strain toward consistency" within institutionalized behaviour.   Max Weber's famous works on religion are an effort to demonstrate the importance of belief systems for the kind of economic system which exists in a society.[4]

It follows from these considerations that it is always possible to ask how any patterned behaviour functions, what role it plays, in supporting or not supporting any other institutionalized behaviour. After the observer sees a certain pattern of behaviour he asks the classic functional question: what is the result of this pattern of behaviour for other patterns of behaviour?   In the study of a Chinese society, a typical question might be: what is the importance or relevance of ancestor worship in the maintenance of the traditional family, village organization and pattern of agriculture?

One sociologist in discussing religion lists six general functions of religion and at the same time indicates some of the limitations of this theoretical framework.

[1.]   Religion, by its invocation of a beyond which is concerned with human destiny and welfare, and to which men may respond and relate themselves, provides *support, consolation, and reconciliation* . . .

[2.]   Religion offers a *transcendental relationship* through cult and the ceremonies of worship, and thereby provides the emotional ground for a new *security* and firmer *identity* amid the uncertainties and impossibilities of the human condition and the flux and change of history . . .

---

4 Discussions of the relationship between belief systems and economic systems are to be found in the following works: Max Weber, *The Protestant Ethic and the Spirit of Capitalism*, trans.   Talcott Parsons (New York: Charles Scribner's Sons, 1958); Max Weber, *Ancient Judaism*, trans. & ed. H. H. Gerth and D. Martindale (Glencoe, Illinois: Free Press, 1952); and Max Weber, *The Religion of China: Confucianism and Taoism*, trans. H. H. Gerth (New York: MacMillan, 1964).

[3.]   Religion *sacralizes the norms and values* of established society, maintaining the dominance of group goals over individual wishes, and of group disciplines over individual impulses . . .

[4.]   Religion may also [in opposition to the previous function] provide standards of value in terms of which institutionalized norms may be critically examined and found seriously wanting . . .

[5.]   Religion performs important identity functions . . .

[6.]   Religion is related to the growth and maturation of the individual and his passage through the various age gradings distinguished by his society. [5]

Yinger points out that those using the functional approach quite often assume that social systems are completely integrated and that every element in the system is functional and indispensable.[6] There is a real question as to whether this is, in fact, true. There may be occasions when an element does not have a function or its function is not operative. When an element does not function or is inoperative its dispensability may be in question. Merton notes these two problems in the first chapter of his book *Social Theory and Social Structure* and in addition points out a tendency to assume that every element has a positive function.[7] Merton attempts to deal with these three problems in his "Paradigm of Functional Analysis" by suggesting that functions may be positive, negative or irrelevant and that within these qualities functions may be either manifest or latent. When he defines a function as being manifest he means: "those objective consequences contributing to the adjustment or adaptation of the system which are intended and recognized by participants in the system." By latent functions he means: "those [functions] which are neither intended nor recognized."[8]

Careful note should also be made of Parsons' comments with regard to functionalism and its use in the analysis of, religion. That is, the functional viewpoint often emphasizes the conservative function of religion and neglects its creative and possibly revolutionary

---

5 O'Dea, pp. 14-15.

6 J. Milton Yinger, *Religion, Society and the Individual* (New York: MacMillan, 1957), pp. 58-59.

7 Merton, pp. 31-33.

8 *Ibid.*, pp. 50-54.

character.[9] The other extreme is also possible. In either case, functionalism becomes an ideological tool rather than a systematic and objective method of analysis.[10]

Another and related problem of functionalism is that it does not account for what Yinger calls "secular alternatives" to religion. From a functional viewpoint, "religion—non-religion is a continuum," and some secular movements have a quasi-religious character.[11] An illustration of this possibility is to be found in Yang's book, *Religion in Chinese Society,* where he devotes a whole chapter to pointing out the quasi-religious character of "secular" communism.[12]

After this brief discussion of functionalism and its limitations, an attempt to define religion and to comment on religion in Chinese society is in order. We start with Yang's definition of religion which combines the structural viewpoint of Wach and the functional viewpoint of

---

9 Talcott Parsons, *The Structure of Social Action,* 2nd ed. (Glencoe, Illinois: Free Press, 1949), especially Part III on Max Weber; Max Weber, "Religious Rejections of the World and Their Directions" in *From Max Weber,* trans. H. H. Gerth and C. Wright Mills, Galaxy Book ed. (New York, 1958) pp. 323-362; and Joachim Wach, *Sociology of Religion* (Chicago: University of Chicago Press, 1944), p. 391. Interestingly enough, the revolutionary character of religion is amply illustrated in the literature on China. Yang in discussing the Qing Period says:

> Except for several uprisings such as that of the twice-renegade Wu San-kuei, when the dynasty was still struggling to establish itself, very few political rebellions of any appreciable proportion were totally unconnected with some religious element or organization.

C. K. Yang, *Religion in Chinese Society* (Berkeley: University of California Press, 1967), p. 219. Yang's contention is supported by Franke, who in discussing the Taiping Rebellion points out the religious influence. He says:

> As we have indicated, the Taipings had a clear, unified, religious-political-social idea, in which they were indoctrinated and for which they fought . . . They saw as their divine task the creation of a heaven on earth for the blessing of all; this held them together and for this they risked their lives.

Wolfgang Franke, "The Taiping Rebellion," trans. Franz Schurmann, in *The China Reader,* Vol. 1: *Imperial China,* ed. Franz Schurmann and Orville Schell (New York: Vintage Books, 1967), p. 188.

10 Merton, pp. 37-46.

11 Yinger, p. 118.

12 Yang, Chapter XIV.

Tillich. Yang states that religion may be seen:

> as the system of belief, ritualistic practices, and organizational relationships designed to deal with ultimate matters of human life such as the tragedy of death, unjustifiable sufferings, unaccountable frustrations, uncontrollable hostilities that threaten to shatter human social ties, and the vindication of dogmas against contradictory evidences from realistic experience. Such matters transcend the conditional, finite world of empirical, rational knowledge, and to cope with them man is impelled to seek strength from faith in such nonempirical realms as spiritual power inspired by man's conceptions of the supernatural.[13]

Some would quarrel with this definition in that it relates religion only to the difficult, unexpected and unexplainable crisis elements of life and leaves out the contribution of religion to the explanation of the meaning, purpose and value of normal human existence. It also suggests a dichotomy between man's thoughts about the natural and the supernatural. As Yang himself points out, the key element in his definition is the supernatural. Such a definition in terms of the supernatural is useful in the functional context.[14] However, some confusion results from his attempt to define superstition as "distinct" from religion. Superstition is:

> an uncritically accepted belief in supernatural powers and its resultant rite; it may be regarded as a part of magic in the sense that it implies not only nonempirical interpretation of natural and human events but also the human attempt to manipulate supernatural forces by either active control or negative avoidance. [15]

The confusion stems partly from the assertion of "dogma" as a part of supernatural religion on the one hand and of "uncritically accepted belief" as superstition on the other. This assertion seems a loose application of "rational" criteria. All supernatural religious belief is non-rational in the sense that it is non-verifiable through reason.[16] A clearer distinction might be found in exploring the

---

13 *Ibid.*, p. 1.

14 *Ibid.*, pp. 1-2.

15 *Ibid.*, p. 3.

16 Non-rationality is fundamental to James' discussion of "the reality of the unseen":

This inferiority of the rationalistic level in founding belief is just as manifest when rationalism argues for religion as when it argues against it . . . Our impulsive belief is here what sets up the original body of truth, and our articulately verbalized philosophy is but showy translation into formulas. The unreasoned and immediate assurance is the deep thing in us, the reasoned argument is but a surface exhibition. Instinct leads, intelligence

manipulative versus non-manipulative aspects, the self-seeking versus self-effacing aspects and the vindication of dogmas "against evidences from realistic experience" compared with vindication of such dogmas in social experience. Going further, Becker's concern with religion as adherence to the "sacred" in traditional societies also stresses emotion over reason.[17]

It might be more useful to think in terms of Weber's concept of rationalization, as discussed by Talcott Parsons, which stresses the reordering of discrete meanings (embodied in symbols), "into a coherent system, an inclusive interpretation of the world as a whole and man's place in it." This process of rationalization, most often the result of crisis situations or the impact of the individual endowed with charisma, is seen as satisfying an " 'immanent' need of the intellect," in Parsons' terms.[18] What is important, however, is the distinction of this process from the inhibiting effects of traditionalism, the diverse elements of which are often incompatible with a rationalized system of beliefs.

---

does but follow . . . Please observe, however, that I do not yet say that it is better that the subconscious and non-rational should thus hold primacy in the religious realm. I confine myself to simply pointing out that they do so hold it as a matter of fact.

William James, *The Varieties of Religious Experience* (New York: New American Library, 1958), pp. 71-73.

17 Howard Becker, *Modern Sociological Theory in Continuity and Change* (New York: Holt, Rinehart and Winston, 1957), pp. 138-184; and Howard Becker and H. E. Barnes, *Social Thought From Lore to Science* (New York: Dover Publications, 1961), pp. 36-37. It seems that Becker would confine his definition of religion to "evaluations bound up with supernaturalism ['the holy']" (Becker, p. 144), allowing for definition of the sacred "deriving from other sources—most generally from an uncritical emotional attachment to those given" values sanctioned by time and culturally transmitted. Here the sacred is primarily derived from the social rather than the supernatural (Becker and Barnes). However, Becker makes this limited definition for analytical purposes vis-a-vis change (Becker, p. 144). In another context, he states (Becker and Barnes, p. 37):

By thus giving heed to sacredness we have in a way anticipated our present section on religion, for there can be no doubt that religion, properly defined, includes both supernaturalism and sacred elements. Indeed, if much value could be granted such evidence, the world's etymologies alone might even lead to the conclusion that the sacred was a more important element than the supernatural in lending it meaning.

Such statements imply a broader definition of religion, given a distinction between the "holy" and the "sacred."

18 Parsons, p. 567.

This distinction in Weber can be stated as that between doctrine and dogma in belief systems. Doctrine, a rationalized system of concepts and distinctive ethics is often, although not necessarily, identified with a priesthood and an institutionalized religious system. Dogma, on the other hand, can be viewed within strict traditionalism as another type of ethical system, "the ultimate warrant of which is taboo."[19] Such "uncritical" beliefs represent the static element of religion and can be associated with non-theological and non-institutionalized systems.

Given this doctrine-dogma distinction, one can acknowledge the great differences in attitudes toward the supernatural (the "idea of God" in Weber's terms) which can range from coercion to entreaty. The complex developments surrounding these attitudes are not important here.[20] But it is helpful to understand that whatever the "critical" nature of these ideas through successive rationalizations, they stem from the same belief elements as those rooted firmly in tradition.

In this study, it seems better to eliminate the term "superstition" altogether, concentrating instead upon the traditional nature of Chinese religion. For these purposes, Becker's division of religion into supernatural and sacred elements would seem to give the distinctions desired by Yang without labelling one as "belief" and the other as "pseudo-belief."[21]

It is not within the purview of this volume to discuss the existence of religion in Chinese society. The authors are acting on the premise that religion exists in Chinese society, and it is necessary to account for it.[22] However, the form of this existence is an entirely different matter. It should be noted that the structural-functional approach allows for at least two structural forms of religion. There is the institutional religion with which the Western world is most familiar, featuring theology, rituals and an organization independent of secular

---

19 Max Weber, *The Sociology of Religion* (Boston: Beacon Press, 1963), pp. 38-39. The use of the word "dogma" is perhaps unfortunate, since dogma is hardly confined to primitive or traditional belief systems. But most fundamentally, it is linked to the static and uncritical nature of beliefs found in Weber's second system of ethics—values as defined through traditional norms.

20 *Ibid.*, Chapter III.

21 See the discussion below on Becker's interpretation of the sacred in religion.

22 For a discussion of this, see Yang, Chapter I.

social institutions. This is not the structural form with which we are dealing in this volume. Rather, we are dealing with a diffused form of religion, with theology, rituals and organization merged with concepts and structures of secular institutions and other aspects of the social order.[23] It follows that separation of religion from other social institutions is nearly impossible. Tönnies has called this form of social organization *Gemeinschaft*.[24]

Becker also deals with sacred-secular phenomena, setting up a continuum of "types" of society ranging from closed-sacred to open-secular (*Gemeinschaft-Gesellschaft*). Sacred and secular attitudes are most broadly defined by an emotional attachment to either the *status quo* (that held to be unalterable and thus sacred), or to change embodied in challenges from both inside and outside the given society (in its most extreme type, resulting in a "pronormless" society verging on break-down). In this respect, "religion" is not coterminous with "the sacred" but is rather a subset of it; its range is restricted to purely supernatural phenomena.[25] This is essentially the position adopted by C. K. Yang in his study and one perhaps difficult to appreciate as part and parcel of religion.[26] As stated above, such restricted criteria do not "speak to" a tradition in which supernatural religion is identified with institutions and a coherent ethical system that intimately link supernatural phenomena with a social milieu and reject any radical severing of supernatural from natural. For the present analysis, religion is defined in a narrower sense and limited to those acts centring on the supernatural, as distinguishable from values traditionally and socially derived. Religious acts so observed can thus appear to have little coherence with a person's social values and conduct, and some people conclude that the Chinese are non-religious. Becker, on the other hand, would probably "type" Chinese peasant societies as strongly sacred and religious in either his narrow or broader definition of this term.

It was pointed out in the preface that the purpose of this monograph is to describe and analyze Chinese religious practices in the Tai Po resettlement area. Descriptive materials require a focus. One

---

23 *Ibid.*, p. 20.

24 Ferdinand Tönnies, *Community and Society (Gemeinschaft und Gesellschaft)*, trans. Charles P. Loomis (East Lansing: Michigan State University Press, 1957), pp. 33-102.

25 Becker and Barnes, *Social Thought* . . . , pp. 36-37.

26 Yang, pp. 1-2.

can describe religion but one must also include the context in which religion is embedded, such as the family, the government and the economic system. By the same token, functional analysis cannot be undertaken without reference to some social system. In this study the family has been chosen as the necessary focus or social system. This choice is justified in the view of the authors by the primary place of the family in Chinese society. The family unit has been basic to much of the activity (i.e., economic, etc.) in Chinese society.[27]

A great deal of the literature concerning traditional Chinese religion deals with the state religion or the so-called classical or "great tradition." This traditional religion was the religion of the Confucianists, the Mandarins, the officials and the scholars. To the reader who is aware of this literature, it will become obvious that only part of what is reported here follows this tradition. We are reporting the religious practices of a remote village people who have undergone a forced migration to an urban centre. Their religion is what has been referred to as the "little tradition" or the religion of the peasant masses.[28] The religious situation of these people may be unique in that they have lived most of their lives in remote villages away from the mainstream of Chinese society. In this respect they are not unlike large numbers of rural Chinese folk all over China. Because of the existence of these enclaves it is impossible to say what "typical" Chinese religious practices are. The descriptive materials which follow can be construed only as indicative of Tai Po resettlement area people. Generalizations beyond this community will have to await further research.

Yang has probably explained the existence of the various religious traditions as well as possible when he notes:

> A relevant point here is the highly eclectic nature of Chinese religion. In popular religious life it was the moral and magical functions of the cults, and not the delineation of the boundary of religious faiths, that dominated the people's consciousness. Even priests in some country temples were unable to reveal the identity of the religion to which they belonged. Centuries of

---

[27] The importance of the family unit is documented in Martin C. Yang, *A Chinese Village* (London: Kegan Paul, Trench, Trübner, 1948); Fei Hsiao Tung, *Peasant Life in China* (London: Routledge & Kegan Paul, 1939); and in other works.

[28] Robert Redfield, *Peasant Society and Culture* (Chicago: University of Chicago Press, 1956), p. 70.

mixing gods from different faiths into a common pantheon had produced a functionally oriented religious view that relegated the question of religious identity to a secondary place.[29]

This explanation simply shows the rather pragmatic view the Chinese take toward religion. It is not hard to reason from this premise that because of the vastness of China and because of the resulting communication problems, various traditions may or may not have been accurately communicated to different areas. But even more important, Chinese religious practices probably depend a great deal on local conditions and the needs of the people both at a given point in time and over a period of years.

---

[29] Yang, *Religion in Chinese Society*, p. 25.

CHAPTER II

LIFE ENVIRONMENTS IN VILLAGE AND RESETTLEMENT AREA *

EARLY HISTORY AND POPULATION

There were six villages spaced around the shoreline of Plover Cove. See Figure I and Figure II for locations. The villages had many things in common: they had all been in place long before the time when the present inhabitants could give an accurate estimate of the actual age of the villages; they were all single-surname, extended clan villages; they were all Hakka 客 家 people; they had for many generations been sending their sons out of the villages to earn a living; and they were all poor.

The word Hakka means "guest" and is used in Hong Kong to refer to a group of Northern Chinese who migrated from the North to Kwangtung 廣東 Province in a series of waves.[1] The dialect of Chinese which they speak is unintelligible to the Cantonese speaking local inhabitants, and as a result of their late migration to the already settled New Territories of Hong Kong, the Hakka people almost inevitably settled on the worst farming land in the Colony, with a general concentration of Hakka people in the northeastern part. Their social customs differ from those of the neighbouring Cantonese

---

* A substantial part of this chapter will appear in revised form as Morris I. Berkowitz, "Ecology and Human Behavior: A Comparison of Rural and Urban Environments and Their Effects on Resettled Hakka Villagers" in *Conservation and Development of the Countryside* (tentative title), ed. J. A. Prescott (Hong Kong: Hong Kong University Press, 1970). This paper was originally presented at the Conference on Development and Conservation of the Countryside held March 15-22, 1969, in Hong Kong.

[1] Lo Hsiang-lin, *Historical Sources for the Study of the Hakkas* (Hong Kong: Institute of Chinese Culture, 1965), pp. 1-32.

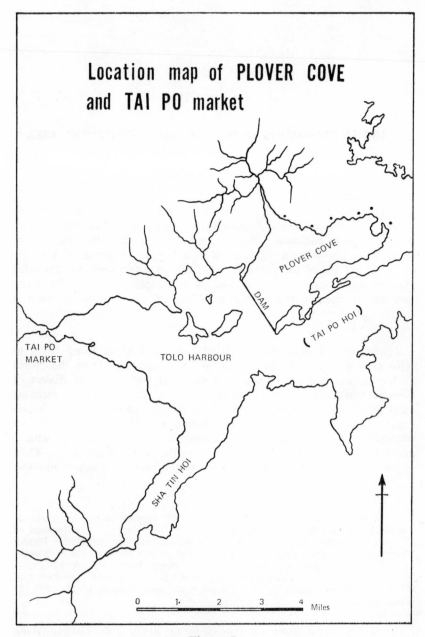

Location map of **PLOVER COVE**
and **TAI PO** market

PLOVER COVE

DAM

(TAI PO HOI)

TAI PO
MARKET

TOLO HARBOUR

SHA TIN HOI

0   1   2   3   4 Miles

Figure I

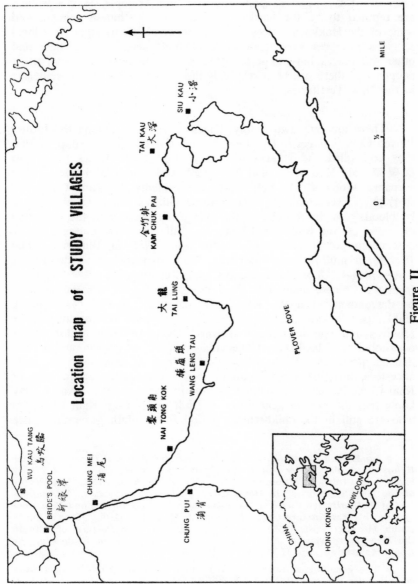

Location map of STUDY VILLAGES

Figure II

(*ben di* 本地 — native) populations.[2] For example, Hakka women are reputed to be the hardest working of all Chinese women, and some of the Hakka practices of ancestor worship and other traditional religious practices vary from those of their neighbours. These and other differences have kept the Hakka socially separated from other people, and there has been relatively little assimilation or intermarriage in the New Territories.

There are only two family names represented among the former Plover Cove villages. The Leis 李 are the dominant group in that they controlled the villages of Chung Pui 涌背, Wang Leng Tau 橫領頭, Siu Kau 小滘, Tai Kau 大滘 and Chung Mei 涌尾 . The surname Wong 王 is held only by residents of Kam Chuk Pai 金竹排 . Every male in each of these villages can trace his descent by blood from the founder of the village. Indeed, with the exception of those of Siu Kau and Chung Pui, all the villagers seem to be descendants of a common ancestor who lived in Wu Kau Tang 烏蛟騰, a multiple-surname village on a plateau behind the Plover Cove villages. The Siu Kau and Chung Pui founding fathers migrated from the Chinese mainland. The Wongs of Kam Chuk Pai seem to be descendants of a Wu Kau Tang ancestor. In any case, among Hakka people individuals with the same surname are assumed to be relatives and intermarriage is frowned upon, although it does occur occasionally. The Plover Cove villagers were all exogamous in their marital practices. Each village maintained a genealogy of male ancestors, boasting a maximum of twelve generations in the case of Kam Chuk Pai and a minimum of nine in the case of Tai Kau.[3] We know that the present generation of adult males from Kam Chuk Pai who are still in the child-rearing period is the ninth generation since

---

2 Lo Hsiang-lin, *et al., Hong Kong and Its External Communications Before 1842, The History of Hong Kong Prior to British Arrival* (Hong Kong: Institute of Chinese Culture, 1963); K. M. A. Barnett, "The People of the New Territories" in *Hong Kong Business Symposium, A Compilation of Authoritative Views on the Administration, Commerce and Resources of Britain's Far Eastern Outpost,* comp. J. M. Braga (Hong Kong: South China Morning Post, 1957); and James Hayes, "The Pattern of Life in the New Territories in 1898," *Journal of the Hong Kong Branch of the Royal Asiatic Society,* II (1962), 75-102.

3 The genealogies of the villages which we used in this project were compiled by the Tai Po District Office during the resettlement project. They were used by the District Office primarily as a means for deciding upon compensation for the villagers.

the founding of the village. If we can assume an average of twenty years between generations, this would indicate that this village was founded between 1761 and 1781.

In 1661 the Manchu Dynasty ordered the removal of all villages from the coastline to a point at least fifty miles inland. This was to contravene the efforts of Zheng Cheng Gong 鄭成功, a senior Ming 明 Dynasty official, to begin a counter-revolution.[4] In 1669 Emperor Kang Xi 康熙 ordered the villages to return to their original sites, and it has been noted in an official document that Wu Kau Tang was one of the villages which returned and was re-established.[5] It is reasonable to assume that the hardship of the move had diminished the population sufficiently to prevent the need for immediate expansion into previously unsettled areas. Within 100 years, however, population apparently began to migrate from Wu Kau Tang to Plover Cove. This may have been the result of over-population on the Wu Kau Tang plateau. Whatever the reason, individuals and their families arrived in Plover Cove at that time. The villages of Siu Kau, Kam Chuk Pai and Wang Leng Tau each seem to have been originally settled by one family. They were followed, perhaps twenty years later, by Chung Mei (founded by a son of the founder of Wang Leng Tau) and Chung Pui, while the last settlers were the founding fathers of Tai Kau. The folk stories of why they came include lack of land in Wu Kau Tang, good hunting and fishing in the new area and a plentiful supply of fresh water from both streams and wells. Whatever the game (probably birds) which originally attracted these migrants was, it has since disappeared and after rather rapid population growth, even the fresh water supply became inadequate in some seasons. Although early in the settlement of Plover Cove there was adequate land for farming, as the population grew farm land became woefully scarce and the population became more and more dependent on fishing in Plover Cove as a source of food.

The census of 1911 showed a total of 583 people living in Plover Cove, with approximately 130 married male heads of households or an average family size of 4.5 people.[6] In 1966 there were 610 people living in Plover Cove in 120 households, making the average family size 5.1. Unfortunately, intermediate censuses do not

---

4 Lo Hsiang-lin, *et al.*, p. 131.

5 *Ibid.*, pp. 135 & 147.

6 *Papers Laid Before the Legislative Council of Hong Kong, 1911* (Hong Kong: Hong Kong Government Press), p. 103.

list the Plover Cove villages separately. Table I gives comparative figures for the populations in the villages in 1911 and 1966. One is struck, however, by the stability of population actually living in the Cove over this fifty-year period, particularly when one recognizes that in 1966 approximately 400 people who are related to the village

TABLE I

Population of Plover Cove Villages, 1911 and 1966

	1911	1966
Siu Kau	90	74
Tai Kau	73	98
Kam Chuk Pai & Tai Lung	93	115
Chung Pui	138	132
Wang Leng Tau & Nai Tong Kok	123	129
Chung Mei	66	62
	583	610

Based on official census data.

occupants and consider themselves villagers were living outside the villages because of the economic conditions. These are the emigrants. The majority of them are in Hong Kong with a few in Britain. Emigration is not a new phenomenon but, in fact, a traditional way of removing excess population from the villages.[7] It would seem from these data that, given the mode of food production and the consumption styles of these villagers, population saturation had been reached at some time prior to 1911. Table II gives a summary of migration. In the generations labelled "5,6,7" in Table II there were eleven male migrants. The eleven known cases, including the founder of Chung Mei, all migrated to local towns within the Sha Tau Kok 沙頭角 area. Most migrated back to Wu Kau Tang. In the generations labelled "4,3,2,1" there were forty-four migrants, most of them migrating

7 Chen Ta, *Emigrant Communities in South China: A Study of Overseas Migration and Its Influences on Standards of Living and Social Change* (New York: Institute of Pacific Relations, 1940).

within the Colony, but quite a few going to other places in Southeast Asia. In the present generation, the migration has been a mixture with both local migration and migration to the West figuring large in the population movement. Other means of population control also appeared in the villages: there were surprisingly large numbers of males who died without leaving issue; marriage was frequently delayed until rather late in a man's life because of inability to provide enough funds for a proper wedding.

The population pressure is further illustrated by the situations which developed during the Japanese occupation of Hong Kong, 1941-1945. Because of failure of food supplies in the urban areas, large portions of the Hong Kong population moved to the New Territories or continued on to China in an attempt to secure a living. The overstrained village economies simply could not absorb this flow of population and starvation was wholesale all over the New Territories.[8] In Plover Cove, the situation was perhaps worse than in the rest of the New Territories since Japanese patrol boats prevented fishermen from pursuing their normal trade. The people ate bark, grass, insects—and many of them died. Both those who lived in the villages and those who tried to move to them suffered horribly.

The poverty of the villages had two fortunate side effects. First, pirates and thieves, who have abounded in South China during the last two centuries, only infrequently molested them. While other New Territories villagers were walling in their more prosperous houses and belongings, the Plover Cove villagers had little to fear. Secondly, their poverty protected them from the incursion of Government, Chinese or British. They were adept at hiding their sons from the Manchus to protect them from being taken away for military service, and their fortunes were so small that Mandarin tax-collectors never bothered to make the long and difficult journey to the villages.[9] However, the villagers feared Government, as they identified it (probably quite accurately) only as a power which took either one's sons or his money. The British also left them alone, except for occasional police patrols and medical service, until the time of the resettlement. In any case,

---

8 James W. Hayes, "The Japanese Occupation and the New Territories," *The South China Morning Post,* December 15, 1967.

9 Rev. Mr. Krone, "A Notice of the Sanon District," *Journal of the Hong Kong Branch of the Royal Asiatic Society,* VII (1967), 104-137, esp. 118-119, 125.

the villagers' attitudes toward Government were formed and remained those of avoidance, basically the philosophy of "Heaven is high, the Emperor is far away."

On August 12, 1959, the Hong Kong Government announced through the press that it was contemplating the construction of a reservoir which, if constructed, would inundate the traditional homes of these villagers, cut them off from the sea and therefore force their removal from the area to a different place of residence. On that same day, the villagers were warned by a Government official, who had gone to the villages to participate in the dedication of a new school, of the possibility of a dam being built and the consequences for their lives. To the villagers, removal was a remote possibility and comprehension of what this would mean to them was beyond the realm of their imagination. It remained this way until December 1962 when, upon the completion of the necessary physical tests demonstrating the feasibility of the project, the Government decided to proceed. It was probably in January, 1963, when a thorough survey of the population of the six Plover Cove villages was undertaken by the Government, that the impending move came into the consciousness of most of the villagers. From then on until November, 1966, when they were physically removed to Tai Po Market 大埔墟, the villagers were immersed in negotiations with the Government. The settlement they received was a generous one.[10]

THE VILLAGES

The Chinese villages of southern Kwangtung Province, of which the Colony of Hong Kong is a southeastern extension, are cast in a similar mould; the Plover Cove villages were no exception to this pattern. The houses are built in straight lines, sharing common walls with other dwellings on either side of an ancestral hall located in the centre of the complex. If the village outgrows the first line of houses because of the limitations of terrain, a second line is frequently built, roughly parallel to the first and behind it. Occasionally, on the death of a father, one or more of his sons may begin a new

---

10 In addition to cash remuneration for their land and property, each male or representative of a male sixteen years or older in the lineage was given a flat in the resettlement area. Each extended family representing four such males was also given a shop space. This was a general formula which was applied, with allowances made in individual circumstances. Further, each village was compensated for village land, and each village was able to negotiate for a "temple" space in the resettlement area.

string of houses at some distance from the original settlement. This occurs for several reasons but usually because of disputes between brothers. The result is a "dispersed" village. Figure III is the housing plan of Chung Pui and illustrates the "dispersed" village but does not contain any second row of houses because of the terrain. Chung Mei, another of the villages studied, illustrated construction with a second row of houses.[11]

The social implications of the kind of village construction revealed in these materials are not simple to draw out. First of all, it must be noted that houses in the villages are all small and crowded. They are almost invariably one and one-half storeys high, with the cock-loft (second storey) covering slightly less than half of the floor area of the ground floor. The cock-loft serves as a sleeping area, usually for the children. The modal house is only ten feet wide and twenty-two feet long. Immediately inside the front door, on one side, is the kitchen with a grass or wood-burning stove, a flat area for food preparation and hooks from the ceiling or walls to hold utensils. It usually has deep covered receptacles for both water and rice. On the other side is a "toilet" area separated from the main house by a wall, with a rock for a seat and a hole through the wall leading to a collection urn, the contents of which are used for fertilization of the fields. Behind this and occupying perhaps two-thirds of the total length of the house is a common room with chairs and tables; this room is frequently also used for sleeping. Then there is another wall and a small sleeping room for the head of the household and his wife. The inside walls of the houses are invariably covered by soot because of the kinds of fuel burned and the inadequate chimneys. Most of the houses were originally built without windows and were dark and grimy. The floors were stone, dirt or concrete. In Plover Cove recent efforts had been made to improve the houses: some windows had been cut through the stone and mud (sometimes cemented over) walls, and some of the coarse red tiles in the roofs had been removed and replaced with transparent plastic tiles. Nevertheless, the houses were dark, dirty, inadequately ventilated and undoubtedly smelly and hard to clean. Figure IV is a drawing of the standard village house.

11 Andrew Boyd, *Chinese Architecture and Town Planning* (London: Alec Tiranti, 1962), esp. pp. 103-108. Although, like similar books, this deals mostly with the houses of the rich and powerful, it also deals in part with peasant houses and is a profitable source for reading on this subject.

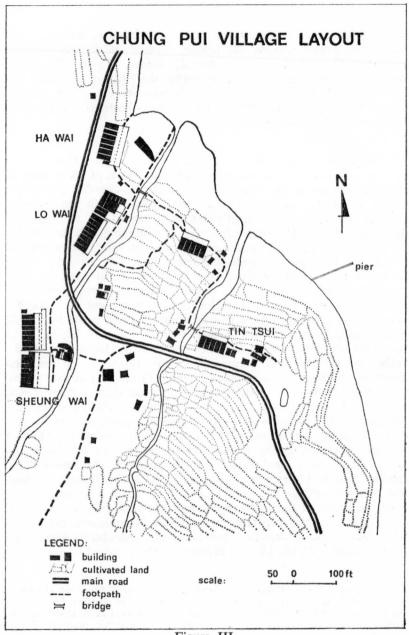

Figure III

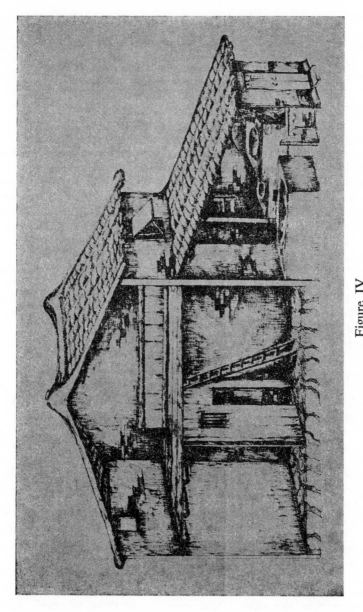

Figure IV

Cut-away Drawing of a Typical Village House

The saving grace of such residences is that, in decent weather, nobody stays in them. They are used primarily for sleeping and cooking, and the life of the villagers takes place outside the houses in the paved courtyard. This spreads out in front of all of the houses and provides a place where work can be done, food-stuffs can be dried in the sun and otherwise prepared, and social life can take place. Withdrawal into the houses occurs only when the weather is poor.

The pattern of social interaction in the Plover Cove villages was conditioned by the availability of this large public area. Since all of the residents of each village had a place on the courtyard and they were all members of the same lineage (these were, after all, single surname villages), they gathered in the courtyard to work, to rest, to chat, to make decisions about village affairs, to continually maintain the intimacy of contact with one another which is so frequently cited as the hallmark of village life. Even those members of the village unable to come out because of age or indisposition lost none of the interaction and attention of the village—a group could congregate before a door and include them in the talk through a slight elevation of the voice. Child care problems became negligible in a physical arrangement like this one, as an aunt, older brother or sister was always available to discipline and control anyone's child who offended the local rules.

It is also true, of course, that this kind of intimacy leads to an intensity of interaction which may magnify and distort conflict and create bitterness, petty quarrels and disagreements rather than harmony. It also strips from the individual any semblance of privacy and makes all of his actions subject to public scrutiny and public praise or condemnation. There is little wonder that the much documented Chinese reticence and modesty developed. The suppression of disagreement in the face of the intimacy of such everyday relationships must have been everyone's goal. The peace and harmony of such small places must have depended much upon the constraint and restraint of all of the members, both adults and children. Indeed, the lack of insight into the costs of intimacy on the part of the children was reported by many men of the villages as having been the root cause of much disagreement and argument.

But other conflicts, more serious than whether someone's child was the aggressor or the victim, also went on in these villages. There was long-standing disagreement about land and who had the privilege of using land. There was jealousy among brothers over whose share of the inheritance was larger or smaller, jealousy among wives as to whose children had the greatest admiration of grandparents, friction among older men about whose authority should be greater or less. All of these potentials for trouble (and many more) were exacerbated by the removal process and frequently flamed into interpersonal feuds between villagers (often brothers) in the presence of Government officials trying to negotiate the removal settlement.

Because of the intimacy of interaction in the village, it was next to impossible for a man to express himself directly and forcefully on the particular issues which were disturbing him. Villagers looked for, and found, ways of attacking one another indirectly and impersonally so as to prevent open conflict and keep the attack on "objective" grounds, thereby enlisting the support of other villagers in the defeat of opponents. It seems to be true, for instance, that arguments about impersonal matters frequently concealed long-smoldering disputes on other issues. Whether this was conscious or not is not discoverable, and perhaps not important, but an illustration would seem in order. One man, a village representative who did not live in the village at all but was a school teacher in a Government school and came back only for weekends, built a charming, large, modern house in 1956.[12] The house had tiled floors and many windows and was attacked by villagers as disruptive of the relationship of the village to its surroundings.[13] The virulence of the attack is hard to explain on these grounds until it is also recognized that the person in question was considered modern, wore Western clothes, did not participate in some village celebrations and had lost almost all other marks of traditional practice. Since his father had sent him out of the community to school as a child (an unusual case), it is likely that the deviance may have had a two-generation history. That so atypical a person was chosen as a village representative (a person selected in villages in the New Territories to represent the interests of the village before the Government) indicates many things, but primarily the recognition by the largely illiterate villagers of their own inadequacies to deal with a

---

[12] This was the only modern house in the six villages, all others being of the traditional village style described in the text. This fact is notable only because in other villages in the New Territories of Hong Kong there are frequently many such houses in any one village—almost all of them made possible by money earned overseas and remitted by faithful sons to their families.

[13] *Feng-shui* will be discussed in Chapter VI.

complex government over life-and-death issues. The selection of their best-educated man for this critical job was an act of wisdom, but not necessarily one which the villagers liked. For solutions to internal problems, they still turned to the traditional older village men rather than to the Westernized, middle-aged school teacher. All these resentments could be objectified and removed from the persons of the people involved and turned into a nonego-involving discourse by talking about houses and house styles, certainly a safer subject than a direct attack on the deviance which was the source of trouble and discontent.

Many men noted that their wives were more frequently involved in open conflicts than they were and held responsible the frailty of women. One suspects that the wives, not related by blood to one another and only adopted members of the village, felt far less constraint in defending the privileges of their own families against the claims of others and in publicly acting out the hostilities and disagreements which their husbands felt (since they were dealing with brothers and cousins) they could not display in public.[14] One recent violent fight occurred in the village rice fields between two women. It is always open to suspicion that husbands, deprived of open acts against one another by their culture and the importance of the family ties, may have taken advantage of the lesser integration of their wives into the village social structure to promote and encourage those open hostilities in which they were denied participation.

The villagers, when all is said and done, were condemned either to live intimately with one another or to make a total break and leave the community. While the former may seem difficult, given the prevailing physical conditions, the latter must have been even more frightening and threatening.

So the peasants held together, lived together, together drew the stuff of life from an unwilling earth. Simple neighborliness, mutual assistance, were obligations inherent in the conditions of things, obligations which none could shirk without fear of cutting

---

14 "In fact, strains and frictions were general in family life. 'Not even a good official can solve family problems' was a popular saying . . . among the mass of the labouring peasants quarrels were the outcome of poverty and excessive toil . . . " David and Isabel Crook, *Revolution in a Chinese Village: Ten Mile Inn* (London: Routledge and Kegan Paul, 1959), p. 7.

himself off from the whole. And that was the community, that the village—the capacity to do these things together, the relationships that regulated all.[15]

Without a family to fall back upon, there is little one can do to protect oneself from the impact of illness, unemployment or other catastrophes. Early life in the village prepared the children to live there effectively, but not anywhere else—at best it prepared them to live in another small village. It was difficult to have the best of two worlds unless one was a male and chose to migrate abroad or to a local industrial city to make a living. Then, at least, one could retain good relations with the family and the village through periodic money remittances which assured one's status as a good son or father and therefore guaranteed one's ability to return to the advantages of the village life when and if one wanted to, without suffering the necessity for living there. Since the distant past, many men have chosen this option.[16]

The villages were crouched next to the sea, crowded from the back by difficult to penetrate, rugged hills and on the front, by a sea which provided both access to the outside world and food when the fishing was good. But the mountains to the rear were also an important resource to the villagers in their marginal economic life. From them came fuel for cooking (grass and twigs), food (berries and roots), medicine (from traditional herbs) and provender for livestock. According to some of the villagers' stories about the origin of the villages, the first migrants came because of the presence of game for hunting in the area, but this source of food has long since been over-hunted and exterminated. The mountains also provided recreation for the children and places to locate the graves of the dead. All in all, they were a substantial resource to the villagers, although perhaps

---

15 Oscar Handlin, *The Uprooted* (Boston: Little, Brown, 1951), p. 12. This quotation is not about Chinese villagers, but about Europeans. We include it to show what we firmly believe: villages around the world, bound up in the same conditions of marginal survival, exhibit startlingly similar characteristics of both social organization and interaction, despite gross differences in the cultural characteristics of the people involved.

16 Dorothy Heid Bracey recently completed a dissertation, as yet unpublished, on the effects of migration on the social structure of Chung Pui. She was gracious enough to provide us with both a copy of the dissertation and various other materials. The fruitfulness of our discussions with her must also be acknowledged. See D. H. Bracey, "The Effects of Emigration on a Hakka Village" (Harvard University Library, 1967).

they did not realize their primary value—they guaranteed isolation and allowed for the maintenance of a traditional way of life which a more exposed position would have made impossible.

Isolation also cut off these villages, like many other Chinese villages, from the mainstream of the development of Chinese religious practices. Removed from the centres of debate and learning, none of these poor villages had ever produced a scholar-official who could have participated in the debates and translated them into meaningful concepts for his fellow villagers. Instead, the villagers got along with the little tradition of Chinese religion, never fully aware of, nor concerned with, the theological and philosophical problems of Confucianism, Taoism and Buddhism. They were particularly aware of the gods which mattered to them—Gods of the fields, of the earth, of the house door, of the kitchen. It was upon these Gods that survival depended and to them that most attention was paid.

It is reasonable to maintain that until 1960 these villages were extremely isolated from the mainstream of life, both Chinese and British. An official Hong Kong Government source says of this area:

> This zone lies on the north coast of Tolo Harbour, the Pat Sin Range forming the western boundary, the eastern boundary following the line of ridges northeast of Plover Cove. The area is remote, mountainous, reasonably well wooded and sparsely populated, the majority of the inhabitants living in the small cultivated coastal strips; one plateau north of Chung Pui is well cultivated. Farming and a little fishing are the sole occupations of the inhabitants.[17]

The villagers could, and did, communicate with other villages in the Sha Tau Kok area, particularly with their relatives in Wu Kau Tang. But to go farther afield offered many problems. To get as far as Tai Po Market required either an arduous walk over difficult terrain on unpaved tracks, crossing unbridged streams which in some seasons were unfordable or the alternative of sailing in a junk which ran from the villages to Tai Po—two hours one way was considered good travel time and four hours against a bad wind was not unusual. Getting to and from the market was an all day excursion; carrying

---

[17] *A Gazetteer of Place Names in Hong Kong, Kowloon and the New Territories* (Hong Kong: Hong Kong Government Press, 1960), p. 193.

goods to sell there was almost impossible unless the goods were small and of high value, precisely what farmers do not have. As a result, commercial vegetable and flower growing, the single most profitable use of agricultural lands in the New Territories, never developed in Plover Cove. Rice was the main crop, and they harvested two crops per year from their marginal fields clinging to the shore, ready to be inundated by salt water any time a good wind stirred up the water. They grew about enough rice from their small land holdings to feed themselves for six months of the year. However, since New Territories rice is considered especially tasty and returns a good price, they did not eat their own rice. Instead, they took their valuable rice and traded it at the market for lower grade, imported rice to stretch the provision as far as possible. Had they had roads (and the necessary diligence), vegetable farming on the same land might well have brought in sufficient income to provide a year's food for the villages.[18]

Fishing had been the other source of income for many years, but since the Japanese occupation (1941-1945), fishing had practically ceased to be a means of livelihood in Plover Cove. The reasons are many, but one may focus for now on the presence of motorized junks in the Colony's fishing fleet, with which the unmotorized junks of the villagers could not compete, and the over-fishing of the waters around

---

[18] The economic marginality of most farmers in the New Territories has been well documented. See, e.g., J. A. Pratt, "Emigration and Unilineal Descent Groups, A Study of Marriage in a Hakka Village in the New Territories, Hong Kong," *The Eastern Anthropologist*, XIII, 4 (June-August, 1960), 147-149. During a small research project in Chung Mei just before removal (September 1966), Lo Hsiang-lin discussed economics with the village representative and summarized his discussion in this way (our translation from the Chinese):

No villagers work for the Hong Kong Government. Very few of them are employed in industry or construction work. Most of them have gone to England to earn a living. The total population of the village is about ninety. Eight villagers are abroad. Occupations vary from running restaurants to working as policemen. Agriculture is the economic base of the village. Farming is mainly done by the women. Even ploughing is carried out by the women. As a result, female villagers do not undertake sewing (or other home industry). Apart from rice, the villagers also produce peanuts and papayas. All are for local consumption. They are not sold on the commercial market.

Professor Lo is Professor of Chinese at Hong Kong University and very kindly made his as yet unpublished materials available to us.

Plover Cove through destructive fishing practices. The villagers themselves made use of "fish bombs" (small explosive charges) which, when exploded in the water, killed or stunned the fish. They then floated to the surface and were picked up. The fact that fry were also destroyed by this practice seemed in the short run to bother nobody, although in the long run fishing ceased to be a useful occupation.

Consequently, a final occupation for men had more recruits—a much higher proportion than ever before of the able-bodied men left the village to work and remit funds home. This development deprived the villages of their young and productive men, created an unusual society in which women, children and old men predominated, and radically affected the whole social structure of the village.[19] With the women working in the fields (as they always had) and the children, watched by old men and women, playing in the courtyard, the scene might look idyllic to the idle passerby, but in fact these villages were dying from the inability to support themselves economically. The steady decline of agriculture in the New Territories over the years had strangled the villages, while the decrease of fishing had been the *coup de grace*. An anthropologist doing a study in Chung Pui slightly before removal comments:

> Among the groups of children playing in front of the houses there seem to be as many boys as girls. But the vast majority of the people in sight are women, whether they are sorting spring onions to take to market or skillfully turning the heavy soil of the paddy fields with the aid of a ponderous water buffalo. If you ask one of the women as to the whereabouts of the men, she will smile and explain that they are away, that Hakka men work out.[20]

By 1960, the situation began to change and the integration of these villages into the Colony began to accelerate. The significant decision to build the dam also provided the villagers with two major improvements in their way of life—a road and jobs. For dam surveying and preliminary work, a road was begun at Tai Po Market to extend, eventually, to the nearby village of Tai Mei Tuk 大美篤 from which the work on the dam face would be conducted. This road was a mere three to five miles from the villages and provided relatively easy access to the Tai Po area, since a truck carrying passengers ran into the market in the morning and back again in the

---

19 See Pratt; see also Bracey.
20 Bracey, pp. i-ii.

evening. Travel time shrank to less than two hours and a trip to Tai Po on Sunday to see a movie or chat in a tea-house became not only a possibility but a pleasure. After the extension of the road, the villagers in cooperation with the District Office set up a ferry service in a motorized junk which plied the waters of the Cove, picking up passengers at each of the villages and carrying them to Tai Mei Tuk. The time to Tai Po shrank to a reliable one and a half hours. Considering the relatively short distance, the time was still rather long, but the reliability was a new feature of village life.

Jobs came more slowly for the villagers. Hakka men are not noted for their willingness to work, in contrast to their known willingness to make their wives extend themselves in the fields.[21] With the rice still being harvested and providing a basic income and the young men working out and sending home money which sufficed for necessities and even an occasional visit to the tea-house or gambling hall, the men, for the most part, still clung tenaciously to their identification as "fishermen" even though their boats were rotting and the amount of time spent on the water was negligible. But as the damming continued, jobs were available and men began to accept them — for the first time they could work out and live in the villages. Wages were good, remittances continued to come from abroad and from sons working in the Colony, and for the first time in anyone's memory the villages enjoyed prosperity.

Even living conditions in the villages improved. Although electricity never came to the villages, running water did. The Government donated to the villagers enough pipe and materials to construct small reservoirs in their streams and pipe the water to stand-pipes in the villages. The pressure in the pipes was not exciting, but the water ran and the shoulder pole with two buckets on the ends used for carrying household water became a thing of the past.

Slowly over these few years, the villagers became more acquainted with life outside Plover Cove. They established relationships with shopkeepers in Tai Po, where they made their purchases and cashed their checks. They became familiar faces on the streets of the market town. Although Kowloon and Hong Kong were still far away from

---

21 Many authors comment on this subject. See Bracey, pp. 5-6; R. Lechler, "The Hakka Chinese," *The Chinese Recorder*, 9 (1878), 352-359; and W. Oehler, "Christian Work Among the Hakkas" in *The Christian Occupation of China*, ed. M. T. Stauffer (Shanghai: China Continuation Committee, 1922).

their normal travel patterns (many villagers had never been there), at least Tai Po began to figure in their daily lives. Even the women went. Many of them, raised in one village and married into another, had rarely, if ever, left the village environment. Now, with their children they were introduced to movies, tea-houses, shops with a bewildering array of goods and the whole furor of urban living. Although this period is hard to estimate, they had perhaps six years, but most certainly three, to look at and become accustomed to the environment to which, in November 1966, they would be moving.

TAI PO MARKET RESETTLEMENT

Tai Po Market is a bustling community of approximately ten thousand people which serves a village hinterland of forty thousand as a marketing, communication, entertainment and social centre. Although many people unfamiliar with the New Territories would find it rather unimpressive as a town, to the Plover Cove villagers the market town represented the modern world. As Groves put it,

> Villages do not, however, exist in isolation from each other. They are bound together by a variety of relationships, the focus of which is usually a market town. The market is the place where important economic transactions occur. But it is much more than this. It may contain a major temple for religious worship. It will provide forms of entertainment not available in villages. If it is a seat of government, various representative groups and associations will have offices there. In its tea houses friends will gossip, disputes will be settled, and the latest political news discussed. The market town is the social and economic center of the area it serves.[22]

The Plover Cove villagers were moved into thirteen five-storey blocks, built especially for them on land reclaimed from the sea and directly facing Tai Po Road (their section of the road was named Kwong Fuk 廣福 or Great Fortune Road), the major connecting road link between Kowloon and the eastern part of the New Territories. They are located literally seconds from bus lines, taxi stands and trucks which regularly ply the routes from Tai Po to anywhere else in the Colony. A few minutes' walk away is the railroad station,

---

22 R. G. Groves, "The Origins of Two Market Towns in the New Territories" in *Aspects of Social Organization in the New Territories,* ed. M. Topley (Hong Kong: The Hong Kong Branch of the Royal Asiatic Society, 1964), p. 16. Market towns in Asia are also analyzed by G. W. Skinner. See his "Marketing and Social Structure in Rural China," *Journal of Asian Studies, XXIV,* 1,2,3, (1964-1965).

approximately thirty minutes from Kowloon with fast, frequent and inexpensive service to that point, the northern New Territories and Canton, China.

The apartment buildings are modern in appearance and are supplied with electricity, running water, indoor plumbing (including flush toilets and showers), fire protection, street lighting and everything else which a modern development project in any part of the world might have, with the possible exceptions of central heating and hot running water, either of which could be inexpensively installed by the villagers. Although the apartments are diminutive, by Hong Kong standards they are not small at all. Each one contains approximately 600 square feet, laid out in a rectangle 36 feet long and 17.25 feet wide, with the kitchen and bathroom, containing an additional 88 square feet, appended on one end. See Figure V.

The apartments are identical in size and have no interior walls except those separating the bathroom and kitchen from each other and from the rest of the apartment. Any further partitioning was left to the discretion of the villagers, using their own design. The apartments all have several large windows and are thoroughly cross-ventilated. The ground floor contains shops (also given to the villagers as part of their compensation) so that no apartments are on the ground floor. Each shop is high enough, however, to easily accommodate a cock-loft.[23] The second floor (first by British reckoning) contains apartments as do the third, fourth and fifth. There is a flat roof on each building, accessible from numerous stairwells. There are no elevators and no internal corridors. This lack is due to the unusual design of the buildings: the apartments on each floor are grouped in pairs, with both doors opening upon a diminutive landing and each landing communicating by stairs to the floors above and below. Therefore, there is a set of stairs for each eight apartments, two apartments on each of four floors. This layout severely restricts potential interaction patterns by reducing to only one family those who can be called next door neighbours and to six other families those who can be reached by walking up or down stairs without going outside. At the time of the distribution of flats, each village was assigned blocks, and within villages the choice of flats was made randomly. Because some families were

---

23 The ground floor is seventeen feet high because the villagers, inundated fairly frequently in Plover Cove, insisted on this height as protection against flooding from typhoon driven waters.

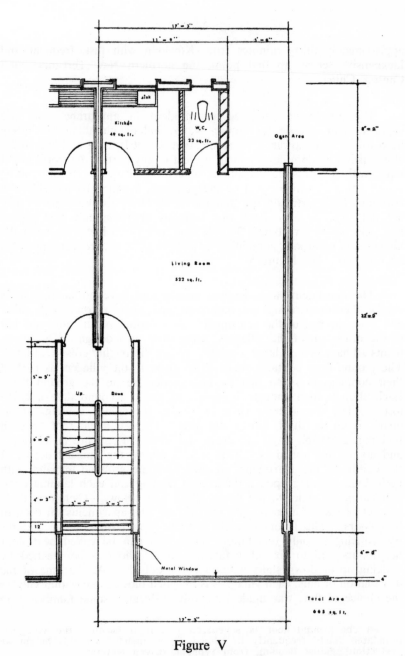

Figure V

Housing Floor Plan for the Resettled Plover Cove Villagers

given more than one flat, it is possible for a family to be surrounded by strangers living in flats which the family is renting out and not to have any former village neighbours nearby.

Figure VI shows the layout of the resettlement area and the location of the original village members in it. There are three squares and a school yard (in addition to internal roads and parking places) which can reasonably be called communal space, but these squares are ill-equipped for use in the way the village courtyards were used. They are small and open to public view, with only a few benches and some children's play equipment. In addition, they are completely open to the weather, without shade or any protection from the stares of curious onlookers or the residents of the apartment houses which surround each square on three sides. Under these conditions it is impossible to regard the squares as substitutes for the courtyards. In addition, of course, lack of easy access to one's residence prevents full use of the square as a place for casual discussion, particularly for housewives who previously could accomplish their household work by ducking in and out of their houses when certain jobs needed to be done.

The location of the school represents a positive addition to the life of the villagers. Formerly there had been two schools, one of which served Siu Kau, Tai Kau, Tai Lung 大龍 and Kam Chuk Pai (Saam Gwong School 三光), while the other served Chung Pui, Chung Mei, Wang Leng Tau, and Nai Tong Kok 泥塘角 (Yuk Kwan School 育羣). In both cases, some village children had to walk long distances over unpaved tracks to get to school, and the children of Chung Pui, one of the largest of the villages, had to ford a stream which often enough was unfordable. The Saam Gwong School, though new, was small with little play space around it; the Yuk Kwan School was old. The school in Tai Po, of course, is within short walking distance for all of the children, has a large, equipped playground and three modern classrooms, and because of its location in an accessible market town has far less difficulty in recruiting qualified teachers. However, although the stimulation of a more cosmopolitan environment may perhaps aid the children's studying, the temptations of movies and other commercial attractions interfere with it. It is also true that in the villages children had work to do tending younger children, helping their mothers in the field, gathering cooking fuel and other chores and that in the resettlement area these responsibilities have diminished, thus freeing more of the children's time for school work. In balance, the change of locale has opened a bigger book of life for the children

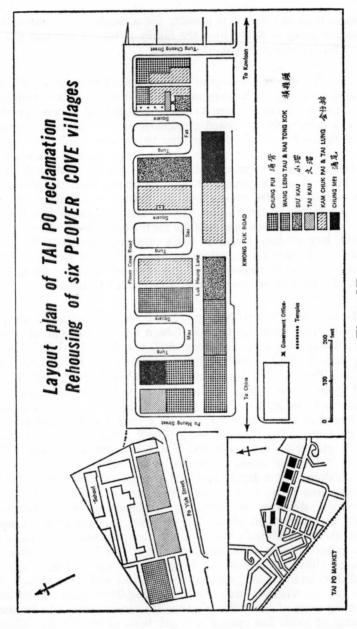

Figure VI

to read, while diminishing their work responsibilities and probably not appreciably affecting the time available for use in school work.

Removal from the soil also removed the people from contact with the sources of their religion. The spirits which were thought to reside in gnarled trees, springs and unusual rocks, and to protect the villagers from drought, disease and misfortune do not fit into a high-rise, concrete world. Before they left Plover Cove the villagers had a ceremony sending these Bo Gong 伯公 back to heaven, acknow-ledging the new world into which they were entering.

Nearness to the open air bazaar in which most Tai Po people shop for their daily food-stuffs and other household necessities has opened an entirely new world for the women of Plover Cove. Every day they can, and most do, go to the market place and buy enough fresh food for the day's consumption in the typical Kwangtung way of not deciding upon menus until one sees what looks "good" that day. Not only does the bazaar furnish for the women possibilities of providing their families with a more varied diet, but it exposes them to the chatter and pleasantries of other Hakka women from Tai Po and the surrounding villages who congregate in this predominantly Hakka market. Their social horizons, formerly limited to the ten or twenty other housewives of the village and perhaps a few others from the neighbouring villages spiced with an occasional arduous trip to a home village, have been remarkably widened. The vendor with whom they bargain as well as the people with whom they rub shoulders are strangers from different life situations and with different perspectives. Whether this situation results in a broadening of perspective is not readily known, but the opportunities for this contact and interpersonal relationships are certainly there for them either to take or to leave as they see fit. Previously, not even the opportunity was available. Within the market they see products which they were not aware of, hear languages which they cannot understand and encounter a bewildering array of stimuli which heretofore they were denied. Whether or not the market affects them may be open to question, but it must have an impact on the development and growth of the children who go with them, dragged by the hand or strapped to their backs. For these children, the socialization of the village can never be duplicated, and they can never be exactly as their mothers and fathers were before them; it is doubtful if they will be even a recognizable image of them.

Similarly, the life space of the younger men and women has been dramatically altered:[24] Hong Kong has become available as it never was before. Without even leaving the family home, they may now experience the fascination of dazzling lights and amusements and have more varied exposure to the dominant ways of life in the Colony. The younger people especially may find the opportunity for higher education and resultant social mobility. Previously, the privilege of greater opportunity was open only to those who moved away from Plover Cove and separated themselves from the villages. Now school beyond the primary grades, technical training and perhaps even a university education are within the grasp of energetic young people. This is not so for the young adults of the village whose education stopped at primary school, if indeed it continued that far: they are a few years beyond the point where the new arrangements can help them. They benefit, however, from the jobs for which they can compete, even though their formerly isolated experiences and lack of secondary education hamper them in the quest for more rewarding positions. Potentially, they represent the most serious problem of the resettlement: with many years to live, they are the last generation socialized in and for village life, and no provision has been made to alleviate their possible problems.

Problems of survival have certainly eased for all members of the villages. Competent medical care is available twenty-four hours every day at well-staffed Government clinics. Houses can be kept clean with far less effort than was necessary to maintain them in a near-filthy state in the village. Interior plumbing, availability of medicines and drugs from nearby stores, including Chinese traditional medicine for those who choose it, have made health a far less troublesome problem than it used to be.

Nevertheless, the changed location has also created problems for the Plover Cove villagers, problems which many did not anticipate but which are directly related to the new physical location. The first of these, of course, is money. As indicated above, although life in the villages was undoubtedly hard, it was also free. Grass and twigs gathered from the hillsides were used for cooking and heating; now fuel must be bought. Water was available from the streams and wells;

24 The use of Kurt Lewin's term indicates, but does not exhaust, our use of his work in this section. See, e.g., his "Behavior and Development as a Function of the Total Situation" in *Manual of Child Psychology*, ed. L. Carmichael (New York: Wiley, 1946).

now a quarterly bill regularly appears. Electricity for lights, fans and rice cookers must be paid for in cash on demand. The amount of money involved is usually small, but for people unaccustomed to budgeting and to the periodic outlay of cash for recurring expenses, the problem is onerous and disturbing. What used to be free now costs money. The hills which once provided meagerly for one's needs are no longer available. The villagers, unaccustomed to living in a totally cash economy and now faced with the necessity for having money available, find the new situation both puzzling and annoying. Their low level of literacy makes the very reading and understanding of bills highly problematic and frequently forces them into the embarassing social situation of having a young child tell his parents or grandparents the contents of these official looking letters. The relevance of his skills in the modern world and the irrelevance of those of his elders are thus pointed up for all to see.[25] This is certainly not a happy situation for the maintenance of respect for one's elders.

The older people suffer much from the intrusion of stairs into their lives. Many of them, capable of walking miles with heavy loads over tracks in the woods, find the stairs inexplicably damaging to their ability to get around. They are almost completely housebound and thus deprived of the comradeship of the other people of their own generation, reduced in many cases to one or two trips downstairs during any given day. Largely stripped of their usefulness, they remain at home for long periods, left out of the new life of the villagers.

SUMMARY

In the interpretation of the religious practices of the former villagers it is vital to remember that they have suffered a dramatic

---

[25] An observer for this project wrote the following concerning periodic bills and the response of one Plover Cove family:

I finished paying the water-rate and returned to the apartment a little while ago. Mrs. Wong knocked at the door saying that Mr. Wong wished to see me. I went to see him right away and told him I had paid the sum. He said he had been worried that the officials of the Water Department might turn off his water supply and was relieved to know that I had paid the water-rate. He recalled that in the old days when he lived in the countryside he did not have to worry about water despite drought. The springs were sweet and clear, unlike the water in the pipe which tastes "medical." The best mountain spring was in Kam Chuk Pai. Since moving to the resettlement area they must not only be bothered with the water-rate but must also worry about the water supply being cut if payment is delayed. Mr. Wong thinks this is truly troublesome and says that he thinks the Government should pay the water-rate.

revision of the environment in which they live. The changes in their physical surroundings have necessarily affected their social existence. As Louis Wirth expressed it, "Whatever else men are, they are also animals, and as such they exhibit the effects of physical aggregation and of their habitat."[26]

Most dramatically, the villagers have exchanged isolation for immersion in a wider, more modern society. From social situations in which they seldom encountered strangers or even neighbours from different villages, they have been plunged into a thriving community which regularly communicates beyond its own borders to places of which these villagers may never have heard. The new life is active and noisy, not slow and quiet.

Perhaps as important, the whole structure of the residential pattern of the villagers has undergone a dramatic change. Whereas formerly they all lived clustered together and shared a communal life based upon kinship and common problems, now they are isolated in much more adequate housing but under conditions which do not allow the previous easy communication with family and neighbours.

> Living in a house also means involuntary membership in a group. The decisions of the architect in designing the house, in laying out the site plan for a group of houses . . . determine to a large extent the nature of the group memberships which will be imposed upon the residents of the houses.[27]

Although the squares in the resettlement area are used for conversation and friendship in the evenings when the sun is down, this limited contact is not equivalent to the ongoing interaction which took place in the village. The degree of intimacy with one's friends and relatives has decreased, allowing for privacy and thus for deviance from the accepted patterns of behaviour, if one chooses to deviate. Although it is dangerous to generalize from the laboratory to the field, certainly the work of Bavelas indicates the significance of position in communication networks and the influence of the physical structure of those networks on the patterns of social interaction.[28]

---

26 Louis Wirth, *On Cities and Social Life,* ed. A. J. Reiss, Jr. (Chicago: University of Chicago Press, 1964), p. 178.

27 L. Festinger, "Architecture and Group Membership," *Journal of Social Issues,* 7 (1951), 152-163, esp. 154. The same point is made in L. Festinger and H. H. Kelley, *Changing Attitudes Through Social Contact* (Ann Arbor, Michigan: Research Center for Group Dynamics, 1951).

28 See Alex Bavelas, "Communication Patterns in Task-Oriented Groups," *Journal of the Acoustical Society of America,* 22 (1950), 725-730.

The change in place of residence has also brought with it a change in the kind of economy which the villagers must practice. Their original village life may have been poor, but their land provided food, their sea provided fish, their hills provided fuel and medicine. What money was available could be used to supplement the gains gathered from a non-cash economy, but even without money, life, no matter how marginal, could continue. Now all these resources are gone and all of life has gone onto a cash basis, or what may be worse, onto a recurring cash basis. Not only is paying for water a new phenomenon, but the recurrent appearance of the bills represents a totally new and uncomfortable experience. The lack of land, to a land-based people, has also caused discomfort although as yet no real problems.

Another aspect of the immersion of the villagers in the market town has been the exposure of the children to a more modern, up-to-date school and their removal from the situations in which previous generations of villagers were socialized. Briefly, they can never be villagers since they will not experience the village way of life except vicariously, through listening to the tales of the old people. The new school and new environment have also introduced to the children a new and more useful language—a language with which they can and must communicate with their teachers and which is much easier to use outside the confines of the resettlement area.

Old occupational skills, which depended so much on the location of the villages, are of no value in Tai Po Market, with the exception of occasional experience gained outside the villages in construction or restaurant work. The villagers are largely trained only to be villagers and their acquired skills do not apply to the new situation. To find rewarding jobs they must find new skills, but to find new skills without fundamental intellectual tools such as reading and writing condemns the newcomers to the lowest rungs of the occupational ladder or to no employment at all.

Village life and village socialization prepared these people for a very limited range of competences in language, in skills of interaction and in responses to the necessities of participating in the economic world. They are special purpose people, totally adequate to the special purposes for which they were originally prepared and indeed, extremely skillful in wresting life from a cruelly barren terrain, but they do not have the fundamental general purpose skills which urban life demands from its successful participants. In these respects they are no different from any rural, peasant people from any place in the world who are dropped abruptly into a life which is not their own. Perhaps the Plover Cove people are a trifle worse off than most others because they did not choose to leave the land and voluntarily migrate but were forced off it by Government practices and policies. However, they are better off than most in that they are economically more fortunate than most voluntary migrants.

CHAPTER III

THE CELEBRATION OF YEARLY FESTIVALS

THE CHINESE CALENDAR

Because traditional Chinese festivals are based upon the Chinese calendar a consideration of the festivals described in this chapter requires an initial understanding of the importance of this calendar, as well as the method by which it is compiled. China has always been an agricultural nation and much of its life necessarily centres on the planting and harvesting of crops. Early in China's history the need for providing guidance to farmers for doing their seasonal work was recognized. Tradition tells us that the calendar dates back to the time of Emperor Yao 堯 [1] who commanded two of his ministers to set up a system for dividing the seasons so that official direction might be given to the people.[2] Throughout more than two thousand years of Chinese history and indeed until the establishment of the Republic of China, setting up the calendar was an official government responsibility: the Emperor himself issued the new calendar each year. As the whole life of the nation was based on the calendar, it followed that any attack upon it was interpreted as tantamount to rebellion.[3]

Although no longer officially recognized, the Chinese calendar is still widely followed. It is made available to the average Chinese in a popular version similar in some respects to the Western almanac. Not only are the months and days themselves listed, but information is also supplied on the inherent characteristics of each month and

---

[1] A legendary emperor who, according to one source, is said to have reigned B.C. 2357-2255. See R. H. Matthews, *Chinese-English Dictionary* (Cambridge, Massachusetts: Harvard University Press, 1945), p. 1090.

[2] Henry Doré, *Researches into Chinese Superstitions* (Taipei: Ch'eng Wen, 1966), IV, 382.

[3] Joseph Needham has discussed the historical context of ideas and techniques surrounding the development of the calendar, emphasizing the marriage of Taoist cosmology, Confucian ethics and Chinese natural science and technology. It is marked by the inseparability in Chinese thought of the physical universe and human (social) phenomena. See Joseph Needham, *Science and Civilization in China* (Cambridge, Massachusetts: Harvard University Press, 1956), II, sec. 13-14, esp. pp. 238-240, 269-270, 357-358. In Volume II of the same study, he discusses the impact of calendrical science on the field of mathematics. In fact, it

day. Advice based on these characteristics is provided on a great variety of such practical questions as what one should do on any given day, where one should go and what one should wear.[4]

The listing of months and days in the Chinese calendar follows a system of dual calculations based upon the movements of both the sun and the moon. The solar year is determined by setting the times of the two solstices and two equinoxes. To these four fixed points in the year are added twenty more, each of which is named after an important agrarian event such as "The Rains" or "Insects Awaken." These twenty-four points in the solar cycle are set in succession at approximately fifteen-day intervals and thus together determine the twenty-four solar divisions or "joints" of the year.[5] The Chinese farmer relies upon these divisions to determine when he should plough, plant, irrigate and harvest.

Although calculations based on the solar year provide guidance for the farmer in his activities, the Chinese calendar itself, in its monthly divisions and progress from year to year, does not follow the movements of the sun but rather those of the moon. The Chinese

---

appears that the manipulation and adjustment of the calendar was practically the only politically and socially sanctioned area for applied mathematics, and this observation can go a long way toward accounting for the lack of development of abstract mathematics. Numerical and symbolic notation were closely linked to concrete phenomena, as well as to the philosophic attitudes relating or explaining these phenomena. "Numbers and things are not two separate entities, and beginnings and endings are not two separate points" (*Sung Yuan Hsüeh An*, Ch. 67, 15a, translated by Forke and quoted by Needham, II, 273). In Needham's words, these preoccupations

> fixed them [mathematicians] irretrievably to concrete number, and prevented the consideration of abstract ideas; but in any case the practical and empirical genius of the Chinese tended in that direction. In the calendrical field mathematics was socially orthodox and Confucian . . . Lastly, a factor of great importance must be sought in the Chinese attitude to 'Laws of Nature' . . . [that] led to a concept of all-embracing Order in which there was no room for Laws of Nature, and hence few regularities to which it would be profitable to apply mathematics in the mundane sphere.

(Needham, III, 150-151). See also III, sec. 19k, "Mathematics and Science in China and the West."

4 For an interesting discussion of the popular Chinese calendar, see V. R. Burkhardt, *Chinese Creeds and Customs* (Hong Kong: South China Morning Post, 1955), Vol. II.

5 For a listing of the twenty-four solar terms, see any major Chinese-English dictionary such as Matthews' *Chinese-English Dictionary* or C. H. Fenn, *The Five Thousand Dictionary* (Peking: College of Chinese Studies, 1940).

have always considered the moon very important and have felt that the listing of months and days in the calendar should follow the lunar cycle. The day of the new moon therefore is always the first day of the month; the full moon always falls on the fourteenth or fifteenth day. Every month in the Chinese calendar has either twenty-nine or thirty days. Of course, the difficulty the Chinese encountered in this system was that twelve lunar months are shorter than one solar year. In order to prevent a succession of lunar New Years which would in time pass through all four of the natural seasons of the year, a modification in the calendar was made to include seven intercalary months in every period of nineteen years. This brought the calendar roughly in harmony with the cycle of the sun. The result is that the Chinese have what Wolfram Eberhard calls a "lunisolar" calendar: [6] the months and days of the calendar are listed according to the lunar cycle; the twenty-four solar divisions are inserted at the appropriate intervals; finally, an adjustment of intercalary months is made to the years, which themselves are made up of lunar months, to bring them into harmony with the cycle of the sun.

The festivals described in this chapter are based upon the Chinese calendar. At the time of the field study one of the Plover Cove villagers was asked to list all of the recognized yearly festivals. The list clearly reflects the lunisolar aspect of the calendar, for it includes festivals based upon both the solar and the lunar cycles.[7] The list also offers a convenient starting point for our study of the yearly festivals. On the one hand, it includes the days marking the beginning of the solar divisions discussed above. This indicates that the villagers who have come from an agricultural environment have followed the example of the traditional Chinese peasant in gearing their lives to the rhythm of the twenty-four solar divisions. Data coming out of our field research indicates, however, that only one of these days was celebrated as a major festival. This is the Qing Ming 清明 Festival which follows the vernal equinox and marks the beginning of the fifth of the twenty-four solar divisions. On the other hand, the list includes eight festivals based entirely on the lunar cycle.

---

6 Wolfram Eberhard, *Chinese Festivals* (New York: Henry Shuman, 1952), p. 37.

7 In his discussion of festivals, Bernard Gallin has superimposed agricultural and religious calendars, calculated according to the lunar calendar. See Bernard Gallin, *Hsin Hsing, Taiwan: A Chinese Village in Change* (Berkeley: University of California Press, 1966), p. 255. This listing gives an idea of the nature and urgency of the villagers' "secular" activities as associated with their religious duties.

No data is available concerning one of these eight, namely, the birthday of Confucius which falls on the twenty-seventh day of the eighth month. Lack of data for this day seems to indicate that the villagers pay little attention to the birthday of Confucius. There is abundant data concerning the remaining seven lunar festivals. One of these, Gold Digging Day, is not so much a yearly festival as an auspicious day to carry out an occasionally necessary task related to ancestor worship. It will therefore be taken up in detail in Chapter VI. The other six lunar festivals together with the Qing Ming Festival, making seven festivals in all, will be discussed in the order in which they are celebrated during the year.[8]

THE NEW YEAR FESTIVAL

Chinese New Year comes on the first day of the second new moon following the winter solstice. For the resettled Plover Cove villagers the celebration begins after several days of preparation and continues on through the fourteenth day of the New Year.

Preparations consist mainly of house cleaning, the purchase of necessary food and equipment for the celebration and the proper decoration of the house. House cleaning requires that the floor be swept carefully and that the furniture be dusted and cleaned. This is in accord with the traditional Chinese idea that the New Year marks a new beginning. Eberhard refers to this preparation as a time "of exorcism, of house cleaning in the material and spiritual senses."[9] The Plover Cove people do not require as much time for their preparations as many did in old China. It is reported that in former days preparations for the New Year often lasted for a whole month.[10] The villagers needed no more than several days.[11]

---

8 Two other festivals are mentioned in the data. The first day of the tenth month is referred to as a Farm Festival at which time the God and Goddess of the Field were worshipped, round dumplings eaten and a family reunion held. Also a Winter Festival is said to have been celebrated at the time of the winter solstice. Lack of information on these festivals would indicate that the villagers did not consider them important and they may have been discontinued. They will therefore not be considered in this monograph. The authors are aware that Confucius' birthday is not normally considered as one of the solar joints. The list we are using is one provided by a villager.

9 Eberhard, p. 9.

10 *Ibid.*

11 Three reasons can be suggested for the decrease in preparation for the New Year. The absence from the villages of a large proportion of the men disrupted the formal public worship of the ancestors so important at this time. In 1966, of 260 adult males, 155 or 59.6% lived

In addition to house cleaning, appropriate lucky sayings are purchased and attached to the sides and tops of main doorways. These are usually written in rhyming couplets and are prominently displayed in the hope that the New Year will be a happy and prosperous one. One villager said:

> We clean the house a few days before the New Year and stick scrolls on the two sides of the door. The scrolls contain lucky words in couplets written in black ink on red paper. Also a paper with the words, "Peace to All Going In and Out," is attached to the top of each doorway.

Pictures of traditional Door Gods are also purchased and pasted on the front door. These are usually drawn on two pieces of paper showing the Door Gods with axes in their hands. The pasting of this paper on the door symbolizes a desire for protection for the family during the year ahead. This practice originated in the story of the faithful ministers of the Tang 唐 Dynasty who posted themselves outside Emperor Tai Zong's 太宗 door at night and protected him from threatening demons. Later, the Emperor ordered that portraits of these warriors be pasted on the palace doors to frighten demons away and eventually the practice spread and became common throughout China.[12]

The celebration actually begins the day before the New Year. Chickens and ducks are killed. A large quantity of pork is prepared and the whole family comes together for a Happy Union Meal. This is served earlier than the normal evening meal, sometimes as early as three in the afternoon but more often around five. If the meal is very early, food may be served again around eight in the evening. In any case, the kitchen is thoroughly cleaned after the meal. Every

---

outside the village. This scarcely avoidable lack of ritual heads raised awkward problems. Second, the collective worship of ancestors was an occasion for the reunification and recognition of lineage unity at the highest level (extending back to the founding ancestors). It could be argued that the small and uncomplicated lineage groups in these villages de-emphasized the "political" factor in the New Year rites—the reassertion of the collective welfare and interests of the lineage over those of competing units. Finally, the poverty of these villagers may have contributed to the decline in elaborate preparation, especially of a wide range of delicacies and decorations. The economic stagnation over such a long period of time may have resulted in a degree of apathy toward occasions celebrating abundance and fertility and expressing the hope of better things to come.

12 For a more detailed account, see E. T. C. Werner, *A Dictionary of Chinese Mythology* (New York: Julian Press, 1961), pp. 311-312.

oily stain is removed and all utensils are made ready for use in the New Year. Also at this time, everyone should wash with green leaf water.[13] This washing is a sign of good luck and symbolizes washing away of the old and welcoming in the new.

For more devout members of the family, this is also a time for paying special respect to the ancestors. This involves a visit to the ancestral hall either on the day of the New Year or on the day before. The visit, however, is not required and the villagers say that worship may just as well take place at home. Local deities such as the Bo Gong and Bo Po 伯婆 together with Tian Hou 天后 and Guan Gong 關公 may also be worshipped at this time.[14]

Family worship plays an important part in the New Year celebrations. Although it is expected that all members will help to make preparation for such worship, it is not necessary for all to participate actively. Family worship includes the offering of fruits to the deities. These fruits are placed on a dish and offered together with the burning of candles and incense. Chickens and ducks are never offered at this time. From the first day to the tenth a red lamp, called the "year lamp," is lit and placed by the door of each home. Care must be taken to see that oil is added frequently so that the lamp continues to burn both day and night. Since resettlement some villagers have replaced the lamp with an electric light which may be switched off at night.

Active celebration in the home usually goes on for five days. On the day of the New Year, people keep to a vegetarian diet, eating such foods as lettuce, dried bamboo shoots and mushrooms. Asked the meaning of this traditional custom, one villager replied: "There is no special meaning. Since we eat only meat dishes on New Year's Eve, we eat more vegetables on New Year's Day." Red packets of "lucky money" (li shi 利市 or more commonly 利是) are given out early in the morning on New Year's Day.[15] The younger people,

---

13 Known in Chinese as lü ye shui 綠葉水, this water is said to be made from the green leaves of the you zi 柚子 or pomelo tree. The leaves are boiled in water, and the liquid produced is believed to have special cleansing power. This practice seems to be exclusively Hakka.

14 Gods are discussed in Chapter IV.

15 The li shi is given as a gift. In Hong Kong, the li shi is an especially important part of New Year celebrations. Children's greetings for the New Year are immediately followed by demands for gift packets: "Gong xi fa cai, li shi dou lai" ("Wishing you happiness and prosperity,

after paying respect to their elders, ask for these packets. People also begin their round of visits to pay respect to their elders, family members and friends, usually in the order of seniority.[16]

On the second day of the New Year the ancestral hall at Wu Kau Tang is visited. One villager described it: "We get up at four in the morning to kill chickens and ducks and make preparation for worship. Most youths go back to Wu Kau Tang and worship there. They go in groups, the more the merrier." Because of the distance involved, elderly people generally stay and worship at home.

From the third day, worship is confined to burning incense every morning at home. The third day of the New Year is called the Day of the Poor Devil. Everyone should stay at home.[17] Apparently it was formerly necessary when going out on this day to take the precaution of first setting off firecrackers in order to scare the Poor Devil away. The question as to whether it is now necessary to do so if, for example, one goes out to dispose of rubbish, was answered, "No."

On the fourth day, the Plover Cove villagers eat special pastries and visit their relatives. Married women visit their families of origin, some of them for as long as ten days, and distribute gifts of pastries and fruits to their relatives. They should also give gifts of pork to their mothers. As it is understood that normal life commences on

---

hand over the lucky money"). *Li shi* gifts are given to children by parents, relatives and married friends. Custom further dictates that any girl still unmarried is eligible to receive the gift, whatever her age. *Li shi* gifts are also given at weddings and other important occasions. However, they are usually given only by older married people. See V. R. Burkhardt, I, 1, 5, 68, 74, 86, 118, 161.

16 Paying respect to one's elders (*bai nian* 拜年) is one of the first ritual duties in the home on New Year's Day. The bowing and paying respect is performed by members of all lower generations to each senior group in descending order, repeated each time for great-grandparents and grandparents. This ritual emphasis on deference to one's seniors also applies to the etiquette of paying calls. One goes out of one's home only to call on those of generational superiority, and returns calls by sending one's children. In this respect, canons of piety also effect a nice division of labour in this social obligation.

17 For Hong Kong's urban residents, the third day seems to be the time for family outings and relaxation—the trains never seem more jammed than on this day as people pour out to the New Territories. The explanation given is that formerly people stayed home on the second day, presumably resting after the strain of New Year's Eve and Day celebrations. But now they spend the first and second days paying and receiving calls, saving the third day to fill as they please. Judging from the public transport system, there seems to be little hesitation about getting out and moving around.

the fourth day, poor families may return to work at this time, although well-to-do families generally continue their celebrations by eating, drinking and having a good time. Many entertain themselves by playing mah-jong. Illiterate women gather around and chat.

On the fifth day, family members make a special effort to say lucky things to each other. One villager told us:

> On this day every member of the family goes out and we say lucky things to one another. We wish middle-aged people prosperity and fruitfulness; we wish children wisdom and alertness; and we wish the elderly comfort and health.

After the fifth day, many continue to burn incense every morning until the fourteenth day when the New Year period comes to an end. Before resettlement the villagers celebrated a Lamp Festival on the fourteenth day. Those families who had male children born during the preceding year invited their relatives and friends to a feast. Specially made lamps were lit and displayed at this time. The custom, however, has been discontinued. The reason given for the discontinuation of the Lamp Festival is that it was believed unlucky: on one occasion a boy died and his death was somehow associated with the lamps. There may have been other reasons as well. No doubt this Lamp Festival was related to and possibly a modification of the traditional festival known by the same name and commonly celebrated in other parts of China.[18]

Everyone, young and old alike, enters enthusiastically into celebrating the New Year. It is a time of eating and drinking, a time of lucky money, a time of relaxation with friends and relatives. Formerly, firecrackers were an important part of the celebration. One woman gave this report: "The New Year after my grandson was born, we fired a whole string of ten thousand crackers, and they cost us over ninety dollars per packet." Since the Government ban on firecrackers, this aspect of the New Year celebration has been discontinued.[19]

---

18 See Eberhard, pp. 62-67.

19 In the fall of 1967, the Government announced a ban on all firecrackers in a general crackdown on the private possession and use of explosives. This announcement came after several months of threats from bombs (always a few real ones among many fakes) planted, for the most part, near police stations, in houses or on the streets.

Another interesting feature of the New Year celebration is the dance of the *qi lin* 麒麟 .[20] The counterpart among the Cantonese is the lion dance. The *qi lin* is a legendary animal whose appearance is regarded as auspicious. The male is the *qi* and the female *lin*. Matthew's dictionary gives the following description of the *qi lin*:

> It has the body of a deer, tail of an ox, hoofs of a horse, one fleshy horn, and the hair on its back is all varied colors, while on the belly it is yellow. It does not tread on the grass, nor eat anything living. Japanese use the term for the giraffe.[21]

At the time of the New Year teams of dancers dress up in the costume of the *qi lin* and perform for the public.

The move from Plover Cove is reflected in consciously recognized changes taking place in the New Year celebration. Because the distance to the ancestral hall at Wu Kau Tang is now greater than before resettlement, the traditional New Year visit is inconvenient, especially for older people. One old lady said, "I used to go, but the distance is too far and I am getting old, so I do not go now." The move to Tai Po has brought a new style of life.[22] Another villager said:

> It is no longer convenient to make certain kinds of pastry now because we lack the essential apparatus. Moreover, it is difficult to gather the whole village together. Now we just sit and chat in groups of two and three.

THE QING MING FESTIVAL

This is the only festival considered in this chapter which is based directly and entirely upon the solar cycle.[23] In the Chinese calendar it marks the beginning of the fifth of the twenty-four annual solar divisions. It comes exactly three and one half months after the winter solstice and consequently, just half a month after the spring

---

20 Translated as "unicorn" in Herbert Giles, *A Chinese-English Dictionary* (Taipei: Ch'eng Wen, 1967), p. 122; or as "monocerous" in O. Z. Tsang, *A New Complete Chinese-English Dictionary* (Hong Kong: Great China Book Co., 1966), p. 955.

21 Matthews, p. 70.

22 The previous chapter discusses some of the ecological factors, particularly the architecture of the apartment blocks and public spaces that interfered with or effectively did away with previous patterns of group interaction.

23 Eberhard, p. 117.

equinox. The Plover Cove villagers estimate the time of Qing Ming by counting one hundred days after the winter solstice. Actually, it usually falls on the one hundred and sixth day after the winter solstice.

Qing Ming is the Chinese spring festival; the villagers often simply call it by this name. It comes early in April of the Western calendar and therefore generally falls close to the time of Easter. The similarities between Qing Ming and Easter have often been pointed out: both are associated with the belief in life after death; Easter emphasizes a belief in resurrection while Qing Ming calls for a sense of obligation to worship one's ancestors; as spring festivals, both convey an emphasis on the idea of new life.

Another name for the Qing Ming Festival is the Zhi Shu Jie 植樹節 or the Tree Planting Festival, similar to what is known in the West as Arbor Day. Years ago the Emperor made it a custom to plant trees in the palace grounds on this day.[24]

In many parts of China the traditional Cold Food Festival is celebrated on Qing Ming. This festival originated with the story of a man named Jie Zhi Tui 介之推 of the seventh century B.C., who on one occasion, cut off a piece of his own leg to feed his starving lord. Later his sacrificial act was forgotten, and in disillusionment he retired to the mountains to live as a hermit. When his lord later called for him he refused to leave the mountains. An attempt to force him out by setting the forest on fire was unsuccessful. His charred corpse was later found and the lord, as a sign of his remorse, ordered that as the man had died on Qing Ming, no fires should again be lit on that day.[25]

Historically, the sources for the Qing Ming tradition go back as far as the early Zhou 周 Dynasty (c. 1000 B.C.). The Zhou rulers were originally nomads from central Asia. After conquering the Shang 商 people of North China, they divided the year into two parts. Winter was spent in the fortified cities in the lowlands. When spring came the tribes moved out to seek food on higher ground. Thus Qing Ming, as a spring festival, was originally associated with the idea of fertility, freedom and love. These origins, though now

---

24 See Burkhardt, I, 24.
25 Eberhard, pp. 117-118.

largely obscure, are closely related to the later development of ancestor worship. Eberhard explains the shift in the significance of Qing Ming as follows:

> Thus the Ch'ing-ming [Qing Ming] festival is an agrarian fertility feast, as we find it in similar form among other nations as well. It marks the beginning of the active, outdoor period of life. The primitive symbolism of love and free union in the fields has given way to the darker aspects of protection of fertility and life through the helpful ancestor spirits; outdoor feasting in a romantic place has become a ceremonial meal at the side of the tombs. A love feast has become the first of three "festivals of the dead." Love songs have all but disappeared and prayers have taken their place. Dances are now unknown; one now kneels down and bows solemnly in front of the tombstone and the altars that have been built there.[26]

Today the Qing Ming Festival is part of the wide-spread Chinese practice of ancestor worship. K. L. Reichelt suggests that ancestor worship manifests itself chiefly in (1) burial practices, (2) worship in the home, (3) the annual sacrifices at the grave and (4) worship in the ancestral hall.[27] Sacrifices are made at the graves of ancestors twice a year, once in the spring on the Qing Ming Festival and once in the autumn at the Chong Yang Festival. In Hong Kong on Qing Ming vast numbers of people make their way to the cemeteries and graves in the New Territories; some even cross the border into

---

[26] *Ibid.*, pp. 126-127; Maurice Freedman, *Chinese Lineage and Society: Fukien and Kwangtung* (University of London: Athlone Press, 1966), pp. 144-154. Freedman would agree that ancestral spirits were positive, benevolent forces that guarded the welfare of the descendants in all matters. Not the least of these matters was fertility, which ensured not only the well-being but the ongoing of the clan. But Freedman notes forms of ancestor worship in other cultures characterized by the exercise of absolute authority by the family head which, while surrendered to the eldest son upon death, is marked by ambiguity with reference to the spirit's ongoing control over the lives of his descendants. Freedman contrasts this idea of the "jural superiority" of such ancestral spirits with the Chinese case: "A Chinese man's estate tends to be dispersed among his sons when he dies and . . . as a dead ancestor he has comparatively little to offer either generally or in the form of support to the few heads of families who follow after him" (pp. 151-152). Thus, he gives equal, if not more, emphasis to the worship of ancestors as a form of respect linking descendants to a common source, which embodies commonly held ideals and values centring on the authority within the family group—this being the essence of filial piety or "obedience." Freedman also mentions an element of commemoration "for its own sake" in the worship of the ancestors.

[27] K. L. Reichelt, *Religion in Chinese Garment* (London: Lutterworth Press, 1951), p. 62.

China. There is great demand for use of all forms of public transport. Lines of people waiting to take the train often extend for a half mile.

The Plover Cove villagers join the crowds in the annual trek to their ancestors' graves. These graves are located in the mountains near Wu Kau Tang. The graves are cleaned and swept, sometimes inscriptions are repainted, and respect is paid to each ancestor. To the question, "What do you take with you when you visit the graves?" an informant replied: "We take candles, offerings and paper money and offer them to our ancestors. Then we pay respect to each ancestor."

THE FIFTH MONTH FESTIVAL

The Wu Yue Jie 五月節 or the Fifth Month Festival is so called because it is celebrated on the fifth day of the fifth month of the Chinese calendar. It is commonly known, especially among Westerners, as the Dragon Boat Festival for the colourful dragon boat races are held each year at this time.

This festival is not regarded as an important one by the Plover Cove villagers. They do not kill chickens and ducks as they do on other festival days. One villager said, "The Wu Yue Jie isn't an important one, so we only make some rice cakes."

The custom of making these rice cakes (zong 粽) originates in the story of Qu Yuan 屈原 , who has been called the father of Chinese poetry.[28] Qu Yuan lived in the southern state of Chu 楚 during the period of the Warring States at the beginning of the third century B.C. At this time the northern state of Qin 秦 was trying to unify China. The king of Chu was unwilling to follow Qu Yuan's advice and was consequently taken captive by the Qin army. Later, in 278 B.C., the capital of the state of Chu was overrun and plundered by the Northerners. As an expression of his great sorrow over this humiliation and his desire to demonstrate his loyalty to his native Chu, Qu Yuan is said to have drowned himself in the river Mi Luo 汨羅 . Tradition says that he drowned himself on the fifth day of the fifth month. When people heard about the tragedy they set out across the river in boats to locate his body. The custom of the annual dragon boat

---

28 See Liu Wu Chi, *An Introduction to Chinese Literature* (Bloomington: Indiana University Press, 1966), pp. 24-34.

races developed to commemorate this event.[29] These races are held in Tai Po as well as elsewhere in Hong Kong each year. Tradition also tells us that at first people threw rice into the water as a sacrifice to Qu Yuan's soul. He is said to have later appeared to a group of fishermen complaining that a river dragon had eaten the rice offered to him. He asked people to wrap their offerings of rice in small pieces of silk tied with silk threads of five different colours. Accordingly, the custom of making rice cakes on the fifth day of the fifth month developed. Glutinous rice is used, and today the cakes are wrapped in leaves tied with tough strands of grass.[30]

It is the custom of the Plover Cove villagers to make the rice cakes and distribute them among relatives. Women frequently visit their homes of origin on this day, taking the rice cakes along as gifts. Asked about worship on this day, a villager said: "We don't do anything special. It is just like the first and fifteenth day of the month. We burn incense and that is all."

THE DOUBLE SEVENTH FESTIVAL

The Double Seventh Festival is based upon the legendary story of the Weaving Maid and the Cowherd which goes back more than two thousand years in Chinese history. In its original form the legend tells of the Heavenly Emperor who loved his beautiful daughter very much. This girl spent all her time by the Heavenly River weaving cloud-like cloth. In time the Emperor felt sorry for his daughter whose life was isolated and lonely, and he married her to a Heavenly Cowherd who lived on the other side of the river. The two fell so deeply in love that the girl completely forgot her loom and the boy his animals. Angered, the Emperor separated the pair, allowing them to meet only once a year, on the night of the seventh day of the seventh month. As the story goes, all the magpies of earth fly to heaven on this night and with their wings form a bridge over the Heavenly River so that the two lovers can come together. They must, of course, be separated again the next day. Thus they

---

[29] For a further description of the dragon boats, see C. A. S. Williams, *Encyclopedia of Chinese Symbolism and Art Motives* (New York: Julian Press, 1960), pp. 138-139.

[30] This is known in Chinese as *nuo mi* 糯米. For a description of local variations in the custom see Burkhardt, I, 27.

remain in the sky and all may see them, for they are the two stars Vega and Altair, one on either side of the Milky Way.[31]

Several versions of this story have developed through the years. In the one which interests people most, the Weaving Maid is the seventh daughter of the Jade Emperor. She was the most beautiful of the seven sisters and no longer able to bear her loneliness, she disguised herself, came to earth and became the wife of a Cowherd. The Jade Emperor was angered and ordered her to return to the Heavenly Court. Unwilling to give her up, the Cowherd followed her all the way back to Heaven. As in the original version, the two were separated and are allowed to meet only once a year across the magpie bridge. The chief difference in this version is that the Goddess came to earth. From this has developed the idea that every year at the time of the Double Seventh she comes to earth and sometimes brings her sisters with her.[32]

The story of the Weaving Maid and the Cowherd appears often in Chinese history and literature. The festival is also called the Qi Qiao Jie 乞巧節 or Entreating Skill Festival. We are told that once on the Double Seventh the imperial consort, Lady Qi 戚, went with the first emperor of the Han 漢 Dynasty to the Pool of a Hundred Sons. Filled with romantic thoughts of the Weaving Maid she made a plait of coloured silk threads. The theme of the silk thread was picked up later by Emperor Wu 武 of the state of Qi who ordered that each year on the Double Seventh the ladies of his court should gather in a special pavilion to try to pass silk thread through a needle's eye. In the Tang Dynasty Emperor Xuan Zong 玄宗 and his favourite, Yang Gui Fei 楊貴妃, celebrated the Double Seventh by pledging to each other their eternal love. It was customary then for court ladies to display fruits, flowers, wine and food as an act of worship to the Weaving Maid and to entreat the Goddess to grant them the skill of embroidery. At that time a young girl's suitability for marriage was largely determined by her skill with a needle and thread. Girls caught spiders and put them into little boxes. If by the next day a girl's spider had spun a web, this was a sign that the Weaving Maid had bestowed upon her the desired skill. Sometimes

---

31 The two stars are known in Chinese as the Niu Lang 牛郎 (Cowherd) and Zhi Nü 織女 (Weaving Maid). For a more detailed discussion of the place of these two stars in the legend see Jin Ling, "Wo Guo De Qing Ren Jie," *Wah Kiu Yat Po*, July 30, 1968.

32 *Ibid.*

a basin of water was exposed to the sun in the middle of the day. Young girls took turns placing needles on the water; the shadow cast by the needle on the bottom of the basin determined whether or not the girl had obtained the skill of embroidery.[33]

Our field study provides information on both Cantonese and Hakka practices connected with the Double Seventh. The Cantonese observe the custom of buying paper articles associated with the Seventh Sister and the Cowherd, including paper dresses, combs, hats and basins. The paper articles are burned as an act of worship on the evening of the seventh. One shopkeeper in Tai Po, lamenting the changing times, told of the way the festival used to be celebrated in Yuen Long 元朗:

> Nowadays things are different. Not very many people maintain the customs. In the old days in Yuen Long and elsewhere there were pageants. The paper basins of the Seventh Daughter were made in huge sizes costing several hundred dollars each.

Besides burning paper articles, the Cantonese make other offerings. Shops remain open, and the following is a description of such offerings in Tai Po:

> In front of the shop I saw a square table on which fruits, cakes, flowers and young plants of grain were displayed. The candles were lit and on the table lay seven cups of tea arranged alternately with seven pairs of chopsticks. In front were some red cosmetics, a mirror, etc., and behind were the fruits including pears, bananas and apples. These were all placed on plates. The burning incense and candles were inserted into tins containing sand. I went there at the time when they had just finished burning the paper basin of the Seventh Daughter. A woman, aged about forty, approached the spot, paid respect to the Gods and worshipped.

The Double Seventh is primarily a festival for women, especially those working in the textile industry who organize themselves into Seventh Daughter clubs with membership fees of three to five dollars per month. Club funds, used to celebrate the Double Seventh, are invested and earn interest. When a member marries she presents a gift of barbecued pork, cakes and fruit to the club. Married members, after the birth of a child, present red coloured eggs to their club sisters.[34]

---

33 Xu Ma Shu Sheng, "Nian Nian Qi Yu Ren Jian Qiao," *Sing Tao Man Pao*, August 1, 1968.

34 "Qi Xi Yu Lan Jian Jin Mang Sha Zha Zuo Gong Ren," *Wah Kiu Yat Po*, July 26, 1968.

It is not clear to what extent Hakka and Cantonese customs are congruent. A certain amount of mixing of customs is inevitable, especially in a situation like Tai Po where Cantonese and Hakka live in the same community. What is clear, however, is that the Plover Cove people carry on very little worship in their celebration of the Double Seventh. The main feature of their celebration is married women's fetching the water of the Double Seventh. The idea of this water, which is said to have medicinal qualities, goes back to a variation on the story of the Weaving Maid: upon returning to earth, the Goddess and in some cases, her six sisters who sometimes accompany her, bathe in the river at dawn.[35] The water in which they bathe takes on special qualities. It is not only fresh and pure but if stored at home for a month can cure sickness and assure long life. The custom among Plover Cove villagers has been for women, on the day of the Double Seventh, to go and fetch water either from the river or from certain wells. The water is taken home, covered in bottles or urns and stored for a month. It is then used in the belief that it contains a special potency. One observer described the way the water is stored.

> She brought me a cup of tea and took me to the kitchen to see the water of the Double Seventh. The water is stored in urns of five pound capacity. These are blue and white and are small at the top and large in the middle. They have usually been used for holding wine. The top of the urn has been carefully stopped with a wooden plug. She said that the water was used for tea and the tea is very refreshing.

For a general description of the custom we have a record of the following conversation between an observer and a villager:

Q. How do you take the Double Seventh water?

A. In the countryside we took the water from wells. Since removal we have taken the water from the well of Pun Chung 泮涌 village near Tai Po or from the river.

Q. What do you do with the water?

---

[35] Cao Yu, "Qi Qiao Jie Za Tan," *Sing Tao Jih Pao,* August 1, 1968; see also Burkhardt, I, 33, for reference to the fetching of water. On the connection between bathing as a purification rite connected with sexual union, see *The New Golden Bough,* ed. James G. Frazer and Theodor H. Gastor (New York: Criterion Books, 1959), p. 315. In the myth, the Goddess would bathe in a stream or river after union with her mortal lover.

A. According to tradition, the water taken on the very day when the Goddesses, the seven daughters of the Heavenly Emperor, descend to earth to play in the water, can be kept fresh and uncorrupted for years. The water has a medicinal effect to cure fevers.

Q. Have you ever tried it?

A. I have.

Q. How do you store the water?

A. It is kept in glass bottles.

Q. Do you know anything about the origin of the Double Seventh?

A. Not in detail. It is said that it is all because of the legend of the Cowherd and the Weaving Maid.

On the day of the Double Seventh, observers met women carrying this water back to their homes. One woman said that over a hundred of the Plover Cove people went to get the water this year, but this seemed strangely few. The custom is that only married women should go for the water, for this is "not the business of unmarried girls."

Indications are that customs surrounding the Double Seventh Festival are changing. Several newspaper sources express concern over the general decline in traditional practices. Double Seventh clubs are becoming rare. Girls are said to be losing interest in the traditional practices. When the Double Seventh comes, they are more interested in "getting together for a day's outing, to breathe in some fresh air and enjoy themselves in the countryside."[36] There is little enthusiasm today for the worship of the seven sisters. "Women of conservative tendency who keep the traditional way of worshipping the Goddesses on the occasion are now as few as the morning stars."[37]

---

[36] "Qi Qiao Jie Ming Jie Lin Bai Xian Zhi Feng Da Jian," *Wah Kiu Yat Po*, July 29, 1968.

[37] "Bai Qi Jie Qing Kuang Leng Dan," *Wah Kiu Yat Po*, July 31, 1968. Numerous anthropologists, among them Gallin and Yang, have stressed the importance of festivals as entertainment and diversion from the monotonous hard labour of agricultural life. The primitive libertinism surrounding fertility that we find in Frazer was quickly muted, if not practically eliminated, in the patrimonial and later Confucian nexus of values, or so say some historical interpreters of Chinese religion. See Max Weber, *The Religion of China* (New York: MacMillan, 1964), pp. 27ff. Nevertheless, C. K. Yang states that festivals were among the few opportunities for men and women to mingle publicly with comparative freedom, the normally applicable public mores being relaxed. C. K. Yang, *Religion*

Many of the Plover Cove women seem to be giving up the practice of fetching the water of the Double Seventh. One woman told an observer that "in the years past women went to the river to collect the water but since we moved to Tai Po this practice has died down." We are told that the younger generation no longer accepts the old beliefs. Several women, when asked whether they had gotten water this year, responded in the same way as the woman who said, "I did not get the river water this year because the water I got last year has not been used up and can still be used this year." The life situation of the villagers has changed and the reactions of individuals to these changes vary. Some carry on the old customs as best they can. Others forget about them. Still others seek for ways to rationalize the changes.[38]

---

in Chinese Society (Berkeley: University of California Press, 1967), pp. 94ff. Gallin emphasizes that festivals were practically the only socially approved way of enjoying better food and perhaps some hired entertainment (Gallin, pp. 39-40). Finally, Baker has pointed out that one mark of initiation into high (i.e., elder) status was the privilege of attending the feast that always followed a ritual, a factor of great importance particularly for the poor. Hugh D. R. Baker, *Sheung Shui, A Chinese Lineage Village* (London: Frank Cass, 1968), pp. 51-54. Given the obvious social importance of festivals in the traditional setting, it is not surprising that this aspect of religious behaviour should easily survive in the face of comparative decline in formal religious rituals. In Tai Po increased recreational facilities are readily available. It is not certain, however, whether the groups of girls who celebrate in Tai Po are together only on these rare festival occasions or whether the groups celebrating at this time follow other divisions within the resettlement area based on proximity and friendship through employment and other such secular distinctions.

38 What appears to be a discontinuation of practice among the older women chiefly because of difficulties and the unfamiliarity of new water sites is for the younger generation an indifference fed by skepticism. Thomas and Znaniecki noted this problem in the Polish immigrant families in America.

But the most complete break between parents and children . . . comes with the emigration of the family as a whole to America. The children brought with the family or added to it in America do not acquire the traditional attitude of familial solidarity, but rather the American individualistic ideals, while the parents remain unchanged, and there frequently results a complete and painful antagonism between children and parents.

William I. Thomas and Florian Znaniecki, *The Polish Peasant in Europe and America* (Boston: Gorham Press, 1918), I, 103-104, 145ff; see also Oscar Lewis, *Tepoztlán: Villagers in Mexico* (New York: Holt, Rinehart and Winston, 1965), p. 83; and Paul J. Campisi, "The Italian Family in the United States" in *Selected Studies in Marriage and the Family,* ed. Robert F. Winch, Robert McGinnis and Herbert R. Barringer (New York: Holt, Rinehart and Winston, 1962), pp. 172-181.

THE FIELD FESTIVAL

Plover Cove villagers celebrate the Field Festival on the fourteenth day of the seventh month according to the Chinese calendar. This has been a harvest festival of thanksgiving during which the Gods of the Field were worshipped with special offerings.

Prior to resettlement one of the main features of this festival was a special feast. A villager described it as follows:

According to the custom of our generation, before we moved out, we used to buy pork, etc. from Tai Po early in the morning on the fourteenth. All the women in the family got up at three o'clock in the morning to make cakes. When we came back before ten o'clock with our pork, they were ready for us to eat. After the chickens, ducks and pork were cooked, they were first presented to the Gods, and then we sat around the table to enjoy our festival meal, usually before noon. According to the customs of my father's generation, they used to buy pork from Tai Po the night before the fourteenth and return immediately by ferry. Sometimes there were villagers who reared pigs. A few days before the festival, they enquired about the amount of pork the people in their village and other villages wanted to buy. Then they killed the pigs and distributed the pork to them early in the morning on the fourteenth according to market price.

Usually several days before the feast the women prepared special cakes not only for their own families but also as special gifts, given with the wish for a happy festival, to relatives and neighbours. Each family used from one to three pecks of rice to prepare these homemade rice cakes.

In addition to the worship of the Gods of the Field and the special feast, this festival provided an opportunity for villagers to discuss problems related to their common welfare.[39] One villager said:

On the festival day, relatives working outside usually returned to the village and if there were problems concerning our welfare to be discussed, we called a meeting at the public house. If there were too many problems, the least important ones would be left to be discussed on the next festival day. If there were no problems, we would have a game of mah-jong or thirteen cards instead of holding a meeting.

---

[39] The integrative function of festivals and ritual for impressing community values and providing a public representation of the collective "ties that bind" is axiomatic in traditional village societies. Malinowski first emphasized the collective interests at stake in *rites de passage*. Bronislaw Malinowski, *Magic, Science and Religion* (New York: Doubleday Anchor Books, 1948), pp. 54ff. Gallin has suggested that interest

Since resettlement some of the villagers have continued to celebrate the Field Festival both by making special offerings at home and by visiting the ancestral hall. An observer visited in the home of a family on the day of the fourteenth and described what he saw:

> There was a small wooden niche nailed on the bottom of the wall. In front of the niche was a table displaying a whole chicken and a piece of boiled pork, both on a plate. Near the plate were small cups of tea and wine. On the other side there were oranges and cakes. In front of the niche of the Earth God were two lighted red candles and some burning incense. Candles and incense were also seen at the door by the entrance. The mother bowed three times to the niche, picked up the offerings and left for the ancestral hall to pay respect.

Several members of the family accompanied the mother. The observer, upon request, was invited to go along. He reported:

> We arrived at the ancestral hall. They welcomed me and fetched a cup of tea. At that time there were four or five people worshipping the Gods. Offerings displayed included chicken, duck, pork, cakes, oranges, wine and tea. Also there were candles and incense and paper silver ingots.[40] The procedure of worship was as follows: after the worshippers lighted their candles and incense they bowed to the altar three times and inserted the candles and incense into the burner; then they displayed the offerings brought with them on the three tables in front of the altar; they concluded their worship by burning paper silver ingots in a specially prepared burner. When they had completed their worship, they picked up the offerings they had displayed, put them back into their baskets and went home. The whole procedure took twenty to twenty-five minutes.

How has the move to Tai Po affected the celebration of the Field Festival? The environment in which the villagers live is no

and participation in festivals (especially the "large shamanistic [sometimes almost orgiastic] rituals") have kept pace with the increasing pressures and demands of urban life and the migration of villagers to Tai Pei or other comparatively distant places. Gallin surmises that these pressures to disperse the village may result in an even greater desire to maintain this "dynamic" means for impressing community values and solidarity, as opposed to the more "sedate" (i.e., more purely ritual-centered) worship of ancestors. Thus in Hsin Hsing, the large community feasts have maintained their vigour and attraction, even for those who live outside the village. See Gallin, pp. 268-269.

40 Known in Chinese as *yin ding* 銀錠 or *yuan bao ding* 元寶錠, these are silver paper ingots burnt for the use of the dead. See Matthews, p. 929.

longer an agricultural one. The Plover Cove people have given up their fields. One villager had this to say: "When we were in the country we worshipped the God and Goddess of the Field. Since we don't have fields anymore we do not worship them." One woman said this about a festival custom in her new life situation: "As every day seems to be a busy festival here, and I have no stone mill, I have not made such cakes to celebrate this festival." The remark is undoubtedly indicative of a change experienced by many villagers. The isolated life in the country was regulated by needs related to farming. The Field Festival reflected the need for enlisting the support of the deities to bring about a good harvest and broke the monotony of life in the village. Tai Po presents a different situation. There is no longer any real need for celebrating a festival based upon concern for a good harvest or for providing diversion from the monotony of village life.

We found no indication that the Field Festival is the same as the Hungry Ghost Festival celebrated by many other Chinese on the fifteenth of the seventh month. One villager said, "Some people say that the fourteenth of the seventh month is the Ghost Festival, and we should offer them something."[41] Asked whether in fact he did offer the ghosts anything, he replied, "No, I used to worship the God and Goddess of the Field. Now I only worship the Earth God." There may be some relation historically between the Field Festival of the Plover Cove villagers and the Hungry Ghost Festival. Eberhard believes that originally the Hungry Ghost Festival may have been a harvest festival and that only after a change caused by Buddhist influence did it take on its present form with emphasis on offerings to the dead. He says:

> Celebrated on the fifteenth day of the seventh month, in late August according to our calendar, it probably was in some places originally a harvest festival; in other regions it was a kind of repetition of the lantern festival of the fifteenth day of the first month, exactly half a year earlier. This is all completely forgotten by now.[42]

In the villages the original emphasis on thanksgiving for a good harvest was not entirely forgotten. Although the Field Festival is celebrated one day earlier than the Hungry Ghost Festival, it may in

---

41 In fact, the Hungry Ghost Festival is celebrated on the fifteenth day of the seventh month.

42 Eberhard, p. 129.

fact carry on the tradition from which the Hungry Ghost Festival developed. There is real question, however, as to how long the tradition will last under the impact of the new environment.

THE MIDAUTUMN FESTIVAL

On the fifteenth day of the eighth month the Chinese celebrate the Midautumn Festival. We are told that it originated in the south-eastern part of China and was a kind of mountain festival. The harvest was over, the granaries full, and people went out to worship the Mountain Gods, at the same time enjoying the beauty of the autumn season. Over the years the emphasis changed and today the festival is characterized by the worship of the moon, the drinking of wine and the eating of moon cakes. Since the moon traditionally stands for the *yin* 陰 or female element in Chinese cosmology, the festival has been chiefly for women. Both preparation for the festival and worship on the night of the festival have been the responsibility of women. Traditionally an altar is built outdoors, either in a court-yard or on a roof. A dish of thirteen moon cakes is placed on the altar—thirteen because this is the number of months in a Chinese intercalary year. In addition to the moon cakes, fruits are also offered.[43] At an agreed upon hour on the night of the festival, the family gathers together, candles and incense are burned and the women take turns bowing before the altar in honour of the moon. When the formalities are over the rest of the night is spent eating and drinking, playing games, telling stories and having a good time.

The customs of the Plover Cove villages follow the general pattern for celebrating the Midautumn Festival. Asked how the festival was celebrated in the country, one villager said:

> The Midautumn Festival is very important. At eight in the evening we used to carry chairs and tables outside the house. We put moon cakes and fruit on the tables and offered them to the moon.

This same villager was then asked why offerings were made to the moon. He said that he did not know, for the villagers simply followed tradition and that according to tradition a certain old man by the name of Zhang 張, who is over 27,000 years old, lives in the moon.

---

43 Traditionally, five fruits: melons, pomegranates, grapes, apples and peaches. "Melons and pomegranates have many seeds, alluding to the great number of children the family would like to have. Apples and grapes symbolize fertility, and peaches longevity." *Ibid.,* p. 104.

Since the move to Tai Po, the celebration is held either on the roof of the resettlement block or in the sitting rooms of individual apartments. A great many moon cakes are eaten. Some villagers believe, however, that those offered to the Gods should not be eaten, for they are poisonous. One of the villagers explained that last year somebody ate such a cake and then became ill.

The most obvious aspect of the festival to an outsider is the preparation, sale and exchange of the moon cakes. They are given to relatives, friends and neighbours. Inasmuch as the cost of purchasing a sufficient number of cakes each year may be considerable, enterprising bakeries organize savings clubs designed to help people prepare for this necessary annual expenditure.[44]   One villager explained:

> We can join a moon cake club. It starts in the eighth month every year. It is either organized by a bakery or an organizer. Any family can join quite freely. They pay three, four, five or six dollars to the organizer every month until the festival. Then they receive their share of moon cakes more cheaply. Otherwise, they would have to spend a lot of money to buy those cakes when the festival comes.

The custom of exchanging and eating moon cakes is almost universal among Chinese in Hong Kong. The following is a good description of these cakes:

> The cakes are enclosed in golden brown pastry, shaped like a small pork-pie, and stamped on top with the emblem of the deity. There are fillings to suit all purses and tastes, the most expensive being seven dollars for a box of four. Confectioners do a roaring trade, and count on clearing their overheads and salaries for the year in the eighth month alone. . . . The basic filling of the moon cake is a sort of cheese composed of sugared beans, lotus seeds, or sesame, ground fine to impart the flavour. In this are embedded ducks' eggs, nuts, or occasionally meat according to the individual taste.[45]

Other customs have been associated with the Midautumn Festival. One villager remembered the days when people lit the traditional Kong Ming 孔明 lantern during the Midautumn Festival. This custom seems to have died out. We are also told that in other villages in

---

44 Burkhardt mentions this practice. Burkhardt, I, 34-35. Such organizations facilitate the same economic foresightedness as that of conscientious Westerners who fortify themselves for the Christmas onslaught by joining year-long Christmas clubs, although such "clubs" meet only financial and not social needs.

45 Burkhardt, I, 53-54.

the Tai Po area, Chinese operas are sometimes performed at this time. In Tai Po itself this is one of the times during the year when the Ma Po 麻婆 Pageant is held.[46] A villager says of the pageant:

> The witch, usually a professional, appears at twilight. Her several female companions are dressed as ghosts and horses. Incense is burned and this attracts the inhabitants, especially children, who follow them all the way to the end. There are also liturgical performances included.

THE CHONG YANG FESTIVAL

The last of the yearly festivals considered in this chapter is the Chong Yang 重陽 Festival. This is also known as the Double Ninth Festival for it falls on the ninth day of the ninth month in the Chinese calendar.

The Chong Yang Festival may have originated among a Chinese ethnic group known as the Yue 越 and may have been related to a harvest festival. Eberhard tells of the custom of going to the mountains or hills on this day and drinking Chinese rice wine mixed with freshly picked chrysanthemums. The suggestion is that there is an "undertone of anguish" here, for "Dangers wait in the valleys where the harvest is going on, and one climbs to the top of the hills to protect oneself by drinking medicine to prevent the unknown pestilences."[47]

Whatever the origins of the festival may be, it is clearly celebrated today as the autumn counterpart of the spring Qing Ming Festival. In fact, it is sometimes simply called the Autumn Festival and has become part of the Chinese cult of ancestor worship. On this day, as on Qing Ming, large numbers of people visit the graves of their ancestors to sweep, clean and redecorate them. Ancestors are worshipped and offerings are made to them. Reichelt says that the Qing Ming ceremonies are repeated, except that white strips of paper used on Qing Ming to decorate the graves are not used on Chong Yang.[48]

---

[46] The pageant is said to be held on the Double Seventh Festival and on the Midautumn Festival. The witch is known colloquially as Ma Po. The name is said to have the same meaning as the more common Wu Po 巫婆 which is the designation for a sorceress or witch. See Matthews, p. 1063.

[47] Eberhard, p. 111.

[48] Reichelt, p. 69.

The Plover Cove villagers invariably associate the two festivals in conversation. The differences between the two were explained in this way:

> It (Chong Yang) is also called the Autumn Festival and is similar to the Qing Ming Festival. We visit the graves of our ancestors. The difference is that several families can go together, whereas at Qing Ming each goes separately.

> At Qing Ming we visit the graves of our nearest ancestors while at Chong Yang we usually visit the graves of ancestors farther apart from our family tie.

In the country, the custom was that people went to the family graves as village groups. A traditional meal of pork and bean curd was served when they returned home. Friends and relatives not in the immediate clan were also invited to share in this meal.[49]

Since resettlement, an attempt has been made to continue this custom but with some modifications. Because of the distance to the site of the graves, a bus is hired for part of the trip. A local restaurant prepares the traditional meal of pork and bean curd which is served when the people return to Tai Po. One villager, with obvious nostalgia, remarked that the homemade pork and bean curd, prepared and served in the country, tasted extremely delicious, but the food in town, although cooked in the same way, had lost the old flavour.

The following are excerpts from villagers' descriptions of the Chong Yang celebrations:

> We now go by motor coach to sweep the graves. Upon our return last year we ordered food from a restaurant and gathered in the open space in Tung Sau 同壽 Square and a nearby store eating as if we were at a picnic. We intend to do the same this year.

> We took the trip to Plover Cove in groups by hired coaches. At about ten in the morning we set off on our journey. Most who went along were young people for they did not need to pay the coach fare. They also obtained two dollars as pocket money. On the journey we ate biscuits, and when we returned we had a meal of bean curd and pork. Because of the lack of cooking facilities to

---

49 For example, daughters who had married men with other surnames could bring their husbands along.

provide food for so many, we are now eating at a restaurant. [50]
On our way to the graves we took along, as usual, those traditional paper gifts for the dead.

The Chong Yang Festival is also the time when the public servant
of each of the villages is expected to make an annual report.   He
must show an account of the income and expenditures of public
money, and make a statement on the balance of funds in the treasury.
A new treasurer may be elected by the people at this time and the
accounts handed over to him.   The task of a public servant, as
anywhere in the world, is not without its frustrations.   One treasurer
said, "It is extremely difficult to do the public business.   I have thought
of resigning, but nobody has been elected to succeed me."

SUMMARY

In studying the festivals reported in this chapter, the overwhelming
impression is not of the strength of traditional religion but of the
inevitability of change.   Whereas once the villagers enjoyed the freedom
derived from being an exclusive community, they now find themselves
a minority group among people with different customs.   Their life,
which was comparatively secure because it was familiar, is now
disturbing because it takes place in new surroundings.   All these
changes have an effect on the villagers' celebration of yearly festivals.
An older village woman, conscious of these changes, said, "In the
country the whole village gathered together on important festivals, but
now each family cooks for itself and people seem to be getting less,
enthusiastic about festivals."

The effect of the change on festivals can be considered at two
levels.   The first is that which results from contact with the people
of the new community in which the villagers now live.   Tai Po is

---

50   The increased wealth of the villagers has apparently increased
the ease and influenced the element of enjoyment of religious occasions,
not only for those who previously took the time and effort for the
preparations and trips but also for the children who are taken along.
Thus, coaches replace the trek on foot, and one goes to a restaurant
instead of preparing special food.   Long excursions are fortified by
additional pocket money and treats; a religious duty which in the village
was also a rare and adventurous outing, still preserves pleasurable
anticipations.   Undoubtedly, a long trip to the graves was a welcome
occasion for a family outing, especially for the women and children, and
the added luxuries now may serve as encouragement to participate in
the traditional observances which may no longer seem special in Tai Po
as they did in the village.

predominantly Hakka but its life is continuous with the larger Cantonese community of Hong Kong.[51]   As time goes on, the villagers' association with the urban community is inevitable.   As familiarity increases, the celebration of festivals will change.   For example, the villagers may gradually adopt the Cantonese practices in their celebration of the Double Seventh.   One may also predict that the Hungry Ghost Festival as celebrated by the Cantonese on the fifteenth day of the seventh month may gradually replace the traditional Field Festival of the Plover Cove people.

The effect of the change experienced by the villagers can be considered at another level.   Their move has been to a wider community. It has been a move into modernity, a move into a world characterized by science and technology.   One may question to what extent any of the traditional festivals survive under the impact of this world's secularizing tendencies.   There is evidence that in the short time since resettlement some customs have already begun to disappear or change their function.   For example, every year fewer women choose to make the long trip to fetch water on the Double Seventh.   The women give various reasons for this, some of them clearly attempts at rationalization.   Within one generation, if not within several years, some customs will probably die out.

It is important to keep in proper perspective the significance of the changes taking place in festival celebration.   Eberhard's comments seem relevant to the experience of the Plover Cove villagers.

---

51   Robert Groves' brief article on the growth of Tai Po village does not give specific figures for the Cantonese-Hakka population ratios in Tai Po and the 1964 figures would have little bearing now.   He does, however, emphasize the foundation for the establishment of Tai Po in the Qi Yue 七約, an association embracing approximately sixty-four villages extending in a semi-circle around the central market in Tai Po and reaching as far as Fanling 粉嶺.   One feature of this political-commercial alliance, formed to provide a new competing market centre, was "that it brought together in a lasting alliance, the Hakka and *ben di* people of the area."   There have always then existed sizable Hakka communities in Tai Po, but the balancing of numbers and the calculation of majorities and minorities in Tai Po proper must be countered by the balance between autonomy and cooperation that was part of Tai Po's origins, and by interests defined within a "greater Tai Po" area, which is increasingly a part of the predominantly Cantonese environment of Hong Kong and the New Territories.   See Robert G. Groves, "The Origins of Two Market Towns in the New Territories" in *Aspects of Organization in the New Territories,* ed. M. Topley (Hong Kong: The Hong Kong Branch of the Royal Asiatic Society, 1964), pp. 16-20.

With changing society, the festivals change too; they lose their
original meanings and take on new ones—sometimes absolutely
different ones. And this change that we are able to observe today
is the same change that has been going on all the time. Because
it is happening before our eyes, we believe it is something extra-
ordinary. It is not a "degeneration." If we use this sentiment-
laden word, we deny ourselves the opportunity of a real understanding of the processes which go on. The change is, rather,
an expression of adaptation to a new social situation, of the
establishment of a new cultural balance in a changing world.[52]

---

[52] Eberhard, p. 145. By a change of meaning we suggest that
what has occurred in the celebration of certain festivals is a shift in
emphasis to recreation. In the apparent commercialization and secularization of such festivals as the Double Seventh, we find celebrations divested
of much of their specifically religious content, particularly with respect
to ritual practice, while still meeting felt social needs for the participants.
In functional terms, this change of content or "meaning" in existent
structures (here religious groups) can be accounted for as an alternative
means of fulfilling a particular function, "just as the same item may
have multiple functions, so may the same function be diversely fulfilled
by alternative items." Robert K. Merton, *Social Theory and Social Structure* (Glencoe, Illinois: Free Press, 1957), pp. 33-34; see also parts seven
and eight of his functional paradigm, pp. 50-54. Merton also raises the
problem of strain and conflict as a result of which existing structures
no longer serve their former function, or cannot adapt to new needs.
A shift in meaningful activity results in breakdown and optimistically,
the emergence of new structures. See part nine of the paradigm, p. 54.
It should be mentioned that problems of subjective "meaning," as Eberhard
uses the term, must not be confused with imputed change of function
in the objective sense. For our purposes, change of content refers to
the kind of activity centered upon ongoing groupings or social arrangements in the social structure—the items under observation—and how
these may change under new influences or in new environments.

CHAPTER IV

THE WORSHIP OF SUPERNATURAL BEINGS

INTRODUCTION

Despite the recognized difficulties associated with an attempt to assign a precise definition to religion, it is generally understood that the term refers primarily to man's understanding of and relationship to that which is both beyond himself and of significant concern to his life.[1] For many Chinese, religion at the popular level has rested upon belief in a world inhabited by a host of both good and evil spirits. These spirits are usually unseen and mysterious, and man's life is in large measure controlled by their activities. J. J. M. De Groot, a great pioneer student of Chinese religion, suggested that this belief reflects a "universalistic animism."[2] Although there are those who have criticised De Groot's work as one-sided in its approach,[3] it has the outstanding merit of being based upon observation of actual practices among Chinese themselves, rather than upon philosophical speculations. Often enough, classic sources on Chinese religion discuss only the beliefs and practices of the elite groups.[4]

---

[1] See Chapter I for a discussion of this problem.

[2] J. J. M. De Groot, *The Religion of the Chinese* (New York: MacMillan, 1912), p. 3.

[3] See W. E. Soothill, *The Three Religions of China*, 3rd ed. (London: Oxford University Press, 1930), p. 21.

[4] See Max Weber, *The Religion of China: Confucianism and Taoism* (New York: MacMillan, 1964); or Joseph Needham, *Science and Civilization in China* (Cambridge, Massachusetts: Harvard University Press, 1956), Vol. II, for emphasis on the philosophy and religion of elite groups, i.e., the "Great Tradition" of the literati. Even De Groot sees a necessary relationship between the philosophical ideas and cosmology of the intellectual tradition and the practices of the peasant (pp. 20-21):

Accordingly the belief in specters is not in China, as among us, banished to the domain of superstition or even nursery tale. It is a fundamental principle of China's universalistic religion; it is a doctrine as true as the existence of the *Yin*, as true as the existence of the order of the world, or the *Tao* itself. But for that doctrine and its consequences, China's cult of gods would appear rather meaningless, and would certainly show itself in forms quite different from those it actually assumes . . . Mental culture and

Among Chinese, the background of the belief in the spirit world seems to have two major sources. The first is rooted in the concept of the general animation of the whole universe which is characteristic of, although not limited to, Chinese thought. Since the universe itself possesses a spirit which pervades and animates all its parts, it follows that not only are men and animals animated, but also plants, together with all forms of what Western philosophers usually regard as inanimate objects.

Second, this universal spirit is thought to be dual in nature. Its positive aspect is its *shen* 神 or *hun* 魂, called by the name of *yang* 陽, which stands for the male principle. Its negative aspect is its *gui* 鬼 or *po* 魄, called *yin* 陰, which in turn stands for the female principle. Because the universal spirit is dual in nature, all lesser manifestations of this spirit fall into a pattern of dualism. The vast pantheon of popular Chinese religion therefore covers both sides of the dualism. Generally speaking, the *shen* are good spirits and the *gui* evil spirits.[5]

The data obtained in this study indicates that the Plover Cove villagers believe in this spirit world and that this belief together with its contingent pattern of worship is central to their religion. Thus, their beliefs lend credence to De Groot's statement that "the study of the relations of the Chinese to their spirit world, and of that spirit world itself, consequently, is a study of their religion."[6] In this chapter we attempt to describe and analyse the evidence of such beliefs.

---

religion have, indeed, been transmitted in China from age to age by tradition; and tradition was always guided by books in which it was written, and the oldest of which are most esteemed.

An opposing view is expressed in the opening sentence to Marcel Granet's study, *La Religion des Chinois:*

L'opposition de la vie urbaine et de la vie rurale est un trait essentiel de la société chinoise ... L'opposition tenait au mode de groupement et au genre de vie: dans des textes, oeuvres des milieux urbains, else s'exprime en termes de sentiment qui veulent suggerer une inégalité de valeur.

Marcel Granet, *La Religion des Chinois* (Paris: Presses Universitaires de France, 1957), p. 1. See also the preface to Vol. XIII of Henry Doré, *Researches into Chinese Superstitions* (Taipei: Ch'eng Wen, 1966), for a discussion of how the Confucian tradition was understood and appreciated by the peasant.

5 For a general treatment, see Kenneth Scott Latourette, *The Chinese: Their History and Culture* (New York: MacMillan, 1964), II, 550-554.

6 De Groot, pp. 20-21.

The religious beliefs and practices of people in any actual situation must be understood as self-contained and consistent for those people. People view their own religion as part of a whole way of life, yet historical and other factors make it possible for us to study Chinese religion at several levels. Howard Smith speaks of an "amalgam of religious beliefs and practices" and suggests that there are four main streams which make up Chinese religion.[7] These are 1) a primitive animism which goes back to the dawn of history, 2) Confucianism, 3) Taoism and 4) Buddhism.[8] We may simplify this analysis by suggesting that the content of Chinese religion has two main sources. On the one hand, there is a folk religion characterized chiefly by a primitive animism and on the other hand, the three traditional religions. Far from being mutually exclusive, these sources have served to complement each other. As for the three religions, some Chinese have always believed that they make up one religion; hence the saying, *san jiao wei yi* 三教爲一 (the three religions are one).[9] The suggestion may be made that Chinese folk religion represents a little tradition, the importance of which has unfortunately been overlooked by many scholars.[10]

Our study indicates that the Plover Cove villagers' belief in a spirit world reflects both the tradition of folk religion and the tradition of the three religions. In this respect they may be typical of rural Chinese elsewhere.[11]

In peasant societies, the tradition-bound perceptions of the entire community govern actions to a high degree. Consistency is linked to reliability, and reflection rarely proceeds beyond recognition and almost automatic response. It is this force of the familiar—a combination of

---

7   D. Howard Smith, *Chinese Religions* (London: Weidenfeld and Nicolson, 1968), p. xii.

8   A great deal of controversy has surrounded the question of whether Confucianism is religion or philosophy. For a good discussion, see C. K. Yang, "The Functional Relation Between Confucian Thought and Chinese Religion" in *Chinese Thought and Institutions*, ed. John K. Fairbank (Chicago: University of Chicago Press, 1957), pp. 268-290.

9   See Doré, Vol. VI, p. iv.

10   See the discussion in Chapter I.

11   A comparison of anthropological studies such as those of Gallin in Taiwan and Graham in southwest China illustrates regional differences. See Bernard Gallin, *Hsin Hsing, Taiwan: A Chinese Village in Change* (Berkeley: University of California Press, 1966); and David Crockett Graham, *Folk Religion in Southwest China* (Washington, D.C.: Smithsonian Press, 1961).

past observations and interpretations that have become tradition-bound—which results in the "consistency" of Chinese religion. This can be more readily appreciated with the breakdown of traditional attitudes:

> But there comes eventually a progressive dissolution of tradition, and at the same time an increase in the number of phenomena which cannot be included in any of the traditional categories, either because they are quite new or because the new interests which have arisen in the community throw a new light upon old classes of phenomena. And the result is a dissociation of attitudes within the community . . . [12]

In either case, the individual must encounter problems of contradiction in his actions. William J. Goode suggests "compartmentalization" as one psychological solution to this problem:

> Socially, role relations tend toward compartmentalization because the individual makes his demands on another and feels them to be legitimate, in specific situations . . . There seems to be no overall set of societal values which explicitly requires consistency or integration from the individual. The process of compartmentalization works mainly by (a) location and context and (b) situational urgency or crises. [13]

---

[12] William I. Thomas and Florian Znaniecki, *The Polish Peasant in Europe and America* (Boston: Gorham Press, 1918), I, 148.

[13] William J. Goode, "A Theory of Role Strain" in *Selected Studies in Marriage and the Family*, ed. Robert F. Winch, Robert McGinnis and Herbert R. Barringer (New York: Holt, Rinehart and Winston, 1963), p. 86. See the entire selection on "Ego's Manipulation of His Role Situation," pp. 86-87, and also Goode's discussion of the term "compartmentalization" as used by Robert Merton and himself (p. 86n). With reference to the context of situation for individual or group actions, Thomas and Znaniecki describe the recognition of the situation by the individual on the one hand and the manner by which his actions may be motivated on the other (pp. 68-69):

> Every concrete activity is the solution of a situation. The situation involves three kinds of data: (1) The objective conditions under which the individual or society has to act, that is, the totality of values . . . which at the given moment affect directly or indirectly the conscious states of the individual or the group. (2) The pre-existing attitudes of the individual or the group which at the given moment have an actual influence upon his behavior. (3) The definition of the situation, that is, the more or less clear conception of the conditions and consciousness of the attitudes. And the definition of the situation is a necessary preliminary to any act of the will, for in given conditions and with a given set of attitudes an indefinite plurality of actions is possible . . . But usually there is a process of reflection, after which either a ready social definition is applied or a new personal definition worked out.

Thus, we can suggest that the objectively observable Chinese religious practices—the mixture of Confucianist, Taoist, Buddhist and popular deities and precepts—derive a great deal of consistency, in a traditional sense, from the "gradual, empirical, unmethodical elaboration of approximately adequate means of control," a control exercised by the close-knit community where "a certain value imposes itself immediately and unreflectingly and leads at once to action."[14]

LOCAL DEITIES

Local deities are those related to a specific locality other than the home. Each village had its own local deities of three different kinds: the Bo Gong and Bo Po or Granduncles and Grandaunts,[15] the Da Wang 大王 or Great Kings (sometimes known as Da Wang Ye 大王爺 or Great King Grandfathers) and the village Tu Di 土地 or Earth Gods.

The Bo Gong and Bo Po were spirits inhabiting mostly fields and trees but sometimes also rocks, streams and roadways. Each village had several of these: one informant said that in walking from one end of his village to the other, one could count eight of these spirits in all. The location of the Bo Gong and Bo Po may originally have been related to some unusual form in nature, such as an especially large tree or a rock with an unusual shape. This phenomenon of identification of unique form with animation has been noted by De Groot.[16] The place inhabited by the spirit was clearly marked, often by a suitable stone with an inscription on it. The Bo Gong and Bo Po were usually located in pairs with the Bo Gong on the left and the Bo Po on the right. One informant pointed out that it was important for the marker to be left out in the open, without fear of exposure to wind, rain or sun, as a demonstration of the power of the spirit to maintain its authority.

The Bo Gong and Bo Po were worshipped as *shen*: they were believed to be basically good spirits who would be willing to provide help for the villagers when such help was needed.[17]

---

[14] *Ibid.*, pp. 2, 68.

[15] See *The Encyclopedic Dictionary of the Chinese Language* (Taipei: The Institute for Advanced Chinese Studies, 1968), II, 928, 933.

[16] J. J. M. De Groot, *The Religious System of China* (Taipei: Ch'eng Wen, 1967), IV, 332ff.

[17] Graham points out, "Certain stones and trees are worshipped as gods . . . " and this seems to be true in many parts of China. However, the Bo Gong and Bo Po are not worshipped as gods but as the residences

There are many different kinds of *shen,* and they have occupied a prominent place in Chinese religion.

> Heaven in the first place has and is a shen, the highest, the most powerful that exists. Shen are also the sun, the moon, the stars. Creating, as they do, the celestial phenomena, thus exercising a mighty influence upon the fate of the earth and of man, those shen are his gods. For the last-named reason, one of man's chief gods is the shen pervading the Earth as a single entity; and those which dwell in its several parts, its mountains, hills, rivers, meres, rocks and stones, are likewise his divinities. Man's gods are also the shen of certain men that people the earth, especially of those that shuffled off their mortal coil, besides those dwelling in animals, in plants, and in lifeless things. [18]

As *shen,* the Bo Gong and Bo Po were relied upon for general protection as well as assistance in time of special need. It was their responsibility to see that the *gui* or evil spirits kept their distance from the village and its fields, and that the well-being of the community was thereby ensured. Their aid was also solicited in times of personal or family difficulty, as when a child became ill. Fortuitous contact with a Bo Gong might lead to remarkable blessings. One villager tells the story of a man who saw a Bo Gong and then won first prize at the horse races. Still, one had to be especially careful how one treated the Bo Gong. A villager gave this example of what might happen through carelessness:

> If anyone sat by mistake on the head of the Bo Gong this would bring bad luck. For example, there was a certain girl who went to take an entrance exam in a certain school. On her way to the school she passed by the stone altar of the Bo Gong and sat on it. Consequently, she failed the exam.

In order to ensure the favour of the Bo Gong and Bo Po, offerings were regularly made to them, usually at the time of such major festivals as the Fifth Month Festival, the Field Festival and the Qing Ming Festival (see Chapter III). These offerings included

---

of spirits and should not be confused with those Graham mentions. See Graham, p. 117. Burkhardt mentions rocks, trees and wells as places which are worshipped but is not at all clear on whether they are themselves gods or are considered the abodes of gods. In one place he says, "Primitive man detected spirits in rocks, trees, and rivers . . . Many of the trees, however, are occupied by friendly spirits." See V. R. Burkhardt, *Chinese Creeds and Customs* (Hong Kong: South China Morning Post, 1955), I, 121-125.

18 De Groot, p. 325.

the burning of incense, candles and joss sticks and the presentation of fish, pork and chicken. Offerings were made both communally and individually; the extent and frequency of such worship was often dependent upon the circumstances prevailing in the village at the time. Occasionally, individuals entered into special relationships with the Bo Gong, characterized by the taking of vows.[19]

Another form of local deity worshipped by the villagers was the Da Wang or Great Kings. Similar in some respects to the Bo Gong, the power of the Da Wang was limited to a given locality. They were also worshipped as *shen* and were believed to be beneficent, maintaining the peace and prosperity of the village, especially as associated with the annual harvests. Senior in rank to the Bo Gong, the Da Wang each had a shrine of his own. These shrines had no roof nor did they contain an image of any kind. As described by one villager, they consisted of a slab of stone with an inscription and an altar at the bottom.

Generally speaking, the Da Wang were worshipped communally at the same time as the Bo Gong with emphasis, however, on the four major solar festivals in the year. A villager described the worship:

> During the quarterly worshipping, each family in the village sent a representative to the Da Wang shrine to have a group ceremony which was called "Honouring the Local Deity." Traditionally, in the seasons of spring, summer and winter, meat was roasted and shared with the attendants after the ceremony. But in the autumn season each would take a piece of meat home to share with his family.

A third form of local deity was the village Tu Di or Earth Gods. These are to be distinguished from their important counterparts, the household Tu Di, which will be considered later in this chapter. The village Tu Di had their altars in the ancestral halls and their sphere of influence covered the whole village. Therefore, responsibility for worshipping them was a communal one.

De Groot points out that the Chinese Earth Gods have traditionally fallen into a general classification of nature spirits, which includes spirits living in mountains and forests, in the water and in the ground.

---

[19] Although Bo Gong and Bo Po are recognized kinship terms, we suspect that their usage here with reference to the abodes of deities is a localized practice, perhaps unique to these villagers.

We are told that this classification was accepted by none other than Confucius himself.[20] Belief in the Earth Gods reflects a recognition of the importance of the soil for the maintenance of life. The soil is the productive part of the universe; hence, the need for fecundation of the soil by the great pervading spirit of the universe is of paramount concern to man and especially man in an agricultural village.

The great changes in the life of the Plover Cove people brought about by the move from village to market town are clearly seen in what happened to two groups of these deities, the Bo Gong and Bo Po and the Da Wang. These deities were intimately associated with the locality which was left behind and the villagers concluded that the deities could not be moved into a new setting. Faced with the problem of what to do with them, the villagers came upon an ingeniously simple and effective solution. All the Bo Gong, Bo Po and Da Wang were sent to heaven. An old man told about it:

> When sending them away we prepared for over a month and invited three or four Buddhist monks to be in charge of the affairs. There was a banquet with pork, bean curd, etc. Each village spent more than a thousand dollars, and all was paid for by the Government.

The person actually in charge of the ceremonies was a geomancer who possessed the necessary qualifications to send the deities away. Apparently, he has given the villagers the guarantee that their deities can be invited back again should the need arise. There is no evidence, however, that the deities have ever been called back. The villagers had faith in the geomancer, although many of the villagers did not seem to understand the ritual which was performed. One informant, asked how the deities could be sent away, replied that he did not know, that the geomancer had just murmured something and then announced that the deities had been sent to heaven.

Indications are that the former local deities of Plover Cove no longer play an active part in the lives of the resettled villagers. The function which these deities served in the old environment is either no longer needed or has been assumed in some other way. One person made the revealing comment that people are now better educated than before. At the time of illness they no longer pray to the Bo Gong but go to a physician instead. At least one person associated sending the deities to heaven with greater religious freedom.

---

20 De Groot, V, 495.

HOUSEHOLD DEITIES

A second category of supernatural beings is that of the household deities—Kitchen Gods, Door Gods and Earth Gods. Other deities associated with the three traditional religions are also often worshipped in the home, but these will be considered later in this chapter.

The Kitchen God or Zao Jun Shen 灶君神 has been common throughout most of China. An altar, plaque or sometimes simply a sheet of paper with an appropriate inscription is attached to the upper part of the Chinese zao 灶 or stove, usually the chimney. Generally neglected during most of the year, he receives special attention just before the lunar New Year, for it is believed that at this time he makes a trip to heaven to give an annual report on the state and activities of the family. Several days before the end of the year, after due worship and offerings, the Kitchen God is taken out of the house, set on fire and sent to heaven. He returns several days after the New Year, at which time he is reinstated with a new image or inscription at his customary location.[21]

Worship of the Kitchen God by the resettled villagers in Tai Po has practically died out. Apparently, many villagers had already either completely discarded the Kitchen God or were doing so by neglect even before resettlement. During removal some of the devout families sent the Kitchen God to heaven for the last time. For others, what remained of the practice of worshipping this deity was left behind in the village. Asked why the Kitchen God could so easily be discarded, one man said the main reason was that in Tai Po the stoves are different. In the village large stone or earthen stoves were used with firewood as fuel, whereas in Tai Po people cook on gas, kerosene or electric stoves. Consequently, there is no appropriate place to attach the Kitchen God. It does not appear, however, that the Kitchen God has been entirely discarded. A few villagers have made the necessary adaptations to the new situation and are carrying on the old practices.

The Door Gods, another type of household deity, are essentially of two kinds. They have been considered fully in Chapter III. Usually the Door Gods are represented by two strips of paper inscrip-

---

[21] For a discussion of the origin of the Kitchen God and various worship practices connected with this deity, see E. T. C. Werner, *Myths and Legends of China* (London: George G. Harrap, 1922), pp. 166-168.

tions which are attached to the centre of the main door of the home at the time of the New Year. They symbolize the desire of the family for protection and blessing throughout the New Year. In time, these paper inscriptions wear off and nothing more is done until the next New Year. A second, more permanent kind of Door God is usually associated with some specific good fortune such as wealth, prosperity or blessing and is represented by a small red plaque on the floor to one side of the entrance of the home. On this plaque is an inscription, identifying this God sometimes as a form of the Tu Di, which may read, Men Kou Tu Di Fu Shen 門口土地福神 (The Blessed Spirit of the Doorway Earth God), and sometimes as an official of heaven with an inscription such as Tian Guan Ci Fu 天官賜福 (The Heavenly Official Who Bestows Blessings). Usually a small container for incense appears in front of this plaque for regular worship.

Although the Kitchen God has for the most part been left behind in the villages, the Door Gods are very much a part of the new life of the resettled Plover Cove people. Possibly the new environment, generally seen as unsuitable for the Kitchen God, on the contrary encourages the worship of a Door God. In a resettlement area, the door of an apartment marks a clear boundary between the home and the outside world. In a strange and often hostile environment the family needs protection. Evidences of this need are easily seen in the heavy iron gates installed in front of nearly every door. Such gates are essential to keep out strangers intent on mischief. The Door Gods represent the desire of the family for both protection and prosperity precisely at the point of contact with the outside world.

A third group of household deities are the Tu Di or Earth Gods. We have already indicated that sometimes they are a kind of Door God. They are usually called Tu Di Shen 土地神, although sometimes also Di Zhu Shen 地主神, and are located in the home itself without necessary reference to the door. Their plaques as displayed by Tai Po people show no images but only an inscription. Undoubtedly, they originated from the close association of the people with their land. De Groot tells of the implications of this association for former generations living in Amoy. Usually negative, these involved taboos against offending the Tu Di for fear of upsetting the relationship of the family to the land and its productive powers.[22] In fact, De

---

22 De Groot, V, Ch. IV.

Groot considers these spirits under the heading of demonology. We have no evidence to suggest that in Tai Po the Tu Di take on this negative quality. They are *shen* and not *gui*. As the villagers move further away from their land, a corresponding change in their understanding of the Tu Di seems likely. The Tu Di are now not so much land deities as apartment deities. They are relied upon for protection and are entreated for blessing and prosperity. Although the responsibility for worshipping them is usually relegated to womenfolk, they are a focal point for the whole family and are viewed as important. One villager made this comment: "In our Tai Po residence there is no tablet of Bo Gong nor a tablet of our ancestors. But there is the tablet of the Earth God. The tablet of the Earth God is a must in family worship."[23]

FORMAL RELIGIOUS DEITIES

A study of the Plover Cove villagers' worship of supernatural beings reflects not only the tradition of animistic folk religion but also the tradition of the more structured and formalized religions. In addition to the local deities and household deities, the villagers also worship supernatural beings associated with Buddhism, Confucianism and Taoism. Three of these are deities of sufficient importance to be considered separately in this chapter.

The first is the Goddess Guan Yin 觀音. It is generally accepted that Guan Yin has evolved historically from the Hindu God Avalokitesvara, an adaption by adherents as a Boddhisatva, who personifies mercy and is said to be the spiritual son of Amitabha Buddha. Avalokitesvara is a male deity who shows his mercy by hearing the prayers of those who call on him, by delivering such persons from their sufferings and by leading them to the Amitabha paradise. It is this deity who was probably introduced into China around the fifth century and given the name Guan Shi Yin 觀世音 or the "One who Hears the Sounds of the World." The Chinese version first appeared in male form, but was later transformed into a female deity.

---

23 Contrast this attitude of the villagers with Freedman's concept of the place of the Kitchen God for worship in the home: "The ritual focus, *par excellence* of the family as a domestic entity is the Kitchen God. Every family has its own hearth, and consequently a separate identity in the worship of that God." Maurice Freedman, "Ancestor Worship: Two Facets of the Chinese Case" in *Social Organization: Essays Presented to Raymond Firth,* ed. Maurice Freedman (London: Frank Cass, 1967), p. 87n.

The exact process associated with this transformation is under dispute by scholars. Doré tells us that the female form began to appear around the seventh or eighth century and by the twelfth century was generally accepted.[24] Undoubtedly, the popular legend of Miao Shan 妙善 contributed much toward establishing Guan Yin as a female deity. Written in A.D. 1102, this story attempted to give a Chinese origin to Guan Yin. Miao Shan was a princess, said to have lived around 2587 B.C. (or, according to another tradition, 696 B.C.), who refused to marry and chose instead to seek to become a Buddha by living a life of contemplation.[25] Opposed by her father, she met with great difficulties only to be saved time and again by miraculous means. Her father was finally converted to Buddhism when she demonstrated her great mercy by sacrificing herself for him. Although the legend did not establish a Chinese origin for the deity, it did associate Guan Yin with the story of Miao Shan, fixed the sex of the deity as female in the minds of the people and provided a concrete object for religious faith. The concept of Guan Yin which the average Chinese has today is defined primarily in terms of the person and life of Miao Shan.[26]

Guan Yin is widely worshipped among Chinese. She is seen as the merciful Miao Shan, willing to offer herself to save those who call upon her. Barondes sums up her place in the Chinese world:

> This goddess is by the side of all in trouble and distress, in danger, in sickness, in senility and misfortune. Her power is unlimited; she sees all, and is able to transform herself into any possible form. If a ship with many persons aboard should be caught in a typhoon, and is foundering, and a single person should call upon the name of Kuan Yin, all aboard could be saved. [27]

The Plover Cove villagers share in this adoration and worship of Guan Yin. In the villages, not only did families frequently set up altars to her in their homes, but her image also appeared in the ancestral hall. Since the move to Tai Po, many families continue to worship her both at home and in public temples. Although she is worshipped primarily by women, there are stories of men who have

---

24 Doré, VI, 200-202.

25 For the complete legend, see *ibid.*, pp. 134-196.

26 This identification has been strongly reinforced by a Chinese film produced by Shaw Brothers (a Hong Kong firm) which identifies Miao Shan with Guan Yin.

27 R. de Rohan Barondes, *China: Lore, Legend and Lyrics* (London: Peter Owen, 1959), p. 30.

sought and received her help.[28]   A villager tells of an experience he
had as a young man.   He was then a smuggler of wine and gun
powder.   One night he had illegal goods on board his ship when he
saw a police launch approaching.   He was afraid and prayed to Guan
Yin to protect him, promising that if she did, he would install a shrine
and worship her forever.   To his amazement, the police launch passed
by without incident, and the villager claims that he has kept his promise.

A second deity of traditional religion popular among the villagers
is Guan Gong.   Known by a dozen different names, the most common
of which are Guan Gong (Duke Guan), Guan Di 關帝 (Ruler Guan)
and Guan Yu 關羽 this deity has occupied a rank equal to that of
Confucius in the official state religion.

Guan Yu was an historical figure who lived during the much
celebrated Three Kingdoms Period.   We are told that he was born
in what is now Shansi 山西 Province in A.D. 162.   As a youth, he
sold bean curd and studied the classics; it is said that he could recite
from memory the Chun Qiu Zuo Zhuan 春秋左傳 .   Later, he met
Zhang Fei 張飛 and Liu Bei 劉備, and the three men took the
famous Oath of the Peach Orchard, pledging to protect each other
and live and die together.   The exploits of the three in service to the
successor to the Han throne have been chronicled in the literary
classic San Guo Zhi Yan Yi 三國志演義 .   Guan Yu was faithful
to his oath, and in A.D. 220 was captured by Sun Quan 孫權 and
put to death.[29]

The process by which this historical figure has been apotheosized
is an interesting subject for scholars.   Doré claims that it is an example
of the process of deification common in China.[30]   During his life,
Guan Yu was praised for his daring feats of courage.   After his death,
numerous honorary titles were conferred upon him and a group of
popular tales and legends became associated with his name.   Hero
worship finally led to apotheosis and in 1594 he was granted the title
of Di 帝 or Ruler.   Because the Manchus believed he assisted them

---

28 See C. K. Yang, *Religion in Chinese Society* (Berkeley: University
of California Press, 1967), p. 11.   Yang points out that Guan Yin
tends to have a fertility function in southern China which is not so
important in northern China.

29 E. T. C. Werner, *A Dictionary of Chinese Mythology* (New York:
The Julian Press, 1961), p. 227.

30 Doré, VI, 78.

in suppressing the Taiping 太平 Rebellion, in 1856 he was given the supreme title of Guan Fu Zi 關夫子 (Great Teacher Guan), and thus an equal rank with Confucius.[31]

Guan Yu has traditionally been worshipped as the God of War. In addition, however, he is the patron deity of literature; this honour was given him because of his reputed knowledge of the Zuo Zhuan 左傳. Today, he is associated with those aspects of life which are of predominant importance to men. His image appears in countless stores, offices and factories.

The Plover Cove villagers associate Guan Gong with Guan Yin, the former being the deity for men and the latter the deity for women. The practice of worshipping Guan Gong which took place prior to removal continues in the resettlement area. Special altars containing his image, with warlike appearance made more ferocious by a face always painted red, are set up in stores and places of business. The shrine usually has either a red electric bulb or a stand for candles and incense, or both. Supplications are made to him primarily for protection and prosperity.

A third deity associated with traditional religion and worshipped by the Plover Cove people is Tian Hou or the Empress of Heaven. Like Guan Gong, this deity seems to have originated in the life of an historic person, though the biographical facts are not at all clear. The Goddess may be the apotheosis of a woman who came from a small island off the coast of Fukien 福建 Province. Her father's surname is variously given as either Lin 林 or Cai 蔡, and she is said to have lived in the eighth, tenth or twelfth century.[32] She is primarily a Taoist deity, although her image often appears with that of Guan Yin in either Buddhist or Taoist temples. The association with Guan Yin is very close. Smith suggests that it is often impossible to distinguish the two.[33] An extensive legend has built up around Tian Hou, the main outlines of which are given by Burkhardt:

> According to the legend, she hailed from Fukien, where she was the daughter of a fisherman. One day, whilst her parents were engaged in earning their bread, she fell into a trance, and dreamed that they were in imminent danger of being overwhelmed by the elements. Running to the beach, she pointed fixedly at their boat

---

31 Werner, p. 226.

32 *Ibid.*, p. 503.

33 Smith, p. 174.

which, alone of all the fleet, safely reached the shore. Since her deification she is credited with curing an Emperor of a disease which defied all the court physicians. [34]

Today Tian Hou is worshipped most of all by the boat people. This is undoubtedly the reason why there is a large temple in her honour in Tai Po and at least one smaller one in the nearby countryside. The connection with fishermen may also account for the Plover Cove people worshipping her. She is known by the affectionate name of Ma Niang 媽娘 (Mother). The villagers worship her either at home or in one of her temples.

Some of the resettled villagers go to the Temple of Ma Niang for the purpose of divination. The usual procedure is to pay respect at the main and side altars by kneeling and placing burning incense sticks in the holders on the altars. The person wishing to choose lots then takes the lots holder from the altar. Returning to his kneeling position, he shakes the lots holder, and with his eyes closed he murmurs and prays that the Gods will make his dream a reality. The lots holder is made of bamboo and is approximately five inches long and three inches in diameter with an opening in the top. With the continued shaking, a lot eventually comes out of the holder. The worshipper picks up the lot and takes it to a temple attendant who exchanges it for a yellow slip of paper. This paper is then taken to an interpreter of divinations who, after referring to a book, tells the worshipper what the Gods' prophecy is. A lot must be chosen for each different matter about which a person wishes to inquire. These lots are classified into three categories: a good lot meaning good fortune, an average lot meaning a future in which a person is not unlucky but does not have an especially fortunate experience and a poor lot predicting bad fortune. Our observer was able to obtain a good lot which read as follows:

> Loss and gain are like prosperity and famine, both are in the hands of Tian 天 (Heaven). If one is happy in nature's way and knows his own destiny, then he shall have security. Those who understand well the meaning of these things will be successful in their endeavors, and their boats will be filled with gold, silver and other goods.

One of the resettlement area women reported the results of picking three lots, one from each of the three classifications. The good lot which she chose assured her that the future would bring

---

[34] Burkhardt, I, 13.

happy events one right after the other. Because this lot was classified as the very best one, she had no reason to worry about the future security of her family. Her son had once chosen an average lot when he went to inquire about his future financial situation. The prophecy was that he would not have any savings although he would not want for money to cover his expenses. She chose a very poor lot when she went to inquire about her husband's blindness: the interpretation of the lot was that the disease was incurable.[35]

Divination is used for almost any question, including education, employment and marriage. One woman inquired as to whether her sister-in-law should lend money. The reply was that the sister-in-law should first make a judgement about the other person's honesty, and if the person was honest, then she should lend him the money.

Reports on the prices paid for the lots varied. One person paid a dollar and ten cents for three lots while another paid only twenty cents a lot. One informant said that strangers might be asked to pay as much as two dollars a lot. Anyone can go to the temple at any time.

At the time of the move to Tai Po, the old images of the Goddess Ma Niang were discarded and new ones were set up in the apartments in the resettlement area. Even though the practice of worship may continue, some villagers seem to have changed in their attitudes toward deities formerly worshipped in the village, including Tian Hou. Some have given up their faith altogether. The following conversation between an observer and an informant seems relevant:

Q. Now that the lights are on, the green floor, the portrait of the Empress of Heaven and the Earth God on the floor look especially nice. Do the portrait and the Earth God have any significant meaning to you?

A. They no longer have any significant meaning. We put them here just because we used to have them in the country. I think it is mere superstition.

Q. If you think this is superstition, you can stop worshipping them, can't you?

A. Oh, it doesn't matter.

---

[35] Actually, the disease was not incurable: the man's eyesight has been partially restored by an operation for cataracts.

Q. What do you mean by this? Do you mean you don't have to worship?

A. It really does not matter.

Q. Are the portrait of the Empress of Heaven and the shrine of the Earth God the same as in your country home?

A. No, we threw them away when we moved here. These are new ones.

Q. Do you have to follow any rites when you throw away the old ones? Is there anything you must avoid doing?

A. No, we simply throw them away.

LOCALIZED CULTS

Temple cults—devoted to a wide variety of such functions as health, fertility, protection and welfare of the local community, economic life, moral order—existed all over China.[36] In rural areas, temples and shrines for the worship of agricultural deities were common. Whether the worship at these shrines was an attempt to manipulate is open to speculation, but for farmers the shrines certainly symbolized the hope that the right combination of natural elements would occur and bring about a good harvest.

The various temple cults had little in common. In Chapter I, we noted that isolation, communication problems, the lack of scholars and sub-cultural differences contributed to heterogeneity in Chinese belief systems. Even among the national cults, names of deities and the functions of the cults varied from one locale to the next.[37] An illustration in the resettlement area is that the Goddess Tian Hou is also called Ma Niang.

In addition to geographical, educational and cultural factors, the functional roles of cults often changed in the course of time. The multi-functional nature of most cults undoubtedly developed in response to the needs of society over a period of years. The fact that a particular function assumed predominance at any given time may suggest social patterns elsewhere in the society. Changes in the relative importance of cultic functions are evident in the history of

---

36 Yang, pp. 1-27.
37 *Ibid.*, pp. 10-12.

the one cult in the resettlement area. This cult's activity is centered in one of the apartments in the resettlement area and is called the Mantis Health School or the Mantis Gymnasium.

The teacher of the Mantis Health School explained that the practices of the cult originated in a Buddhist monastery, the Temple of Bamboo Wood, in Kiangsi 江西 Province. The cult's system has been passed from teacher to pupil for several generations. According to one informant, the cult was founded in the Plover Cove villages to teach the art of self-defence (so that the villagers could protect themselves against pirates and strangers) and physical fitness. However, self-defence and physical fitness were not the only functions the cult served in the history of the villages. Members of the cult also provided a *qi lin* dance team which performed at village festivities, and the teacher was a Chinese herbalist who provided traditional Chinese medicines. In the more recent past, when self-defence against outside intruders was not a particular problem in the villages, the emphasis shifted to cultural, artistic, recreational and medical functions. In the resettlement area, the cult has retained these functions despite the impact of the urban environment and availability of Western medicine. The cult now functions as a focus for social gatherings and activities.[38] Pupils frequently gather on the premises to play recordings of Mandarin pop songs and chat.

This particular cult has a formalized and printed set of rules and regulations. Among other things, the rules of the cult demand that the pupils show unconditional respect for the teacher and that they love and help each other. Additionally, as individuals and as a group, the pupils are to protect the honour of the cult. The students are to use the arts they learn only for purposes of self-defence; violation of this rule results in their dismissal from the school.

Great stress is placed on being a good gymnast and having emotional control. One of the observers asked the teacher about an attack known as "hitting the vital point," and whether or not it is taught. He replied:

> Indeed, it is a very serious attack. After hitting a person, he will die in a calculated number of hours. Before one learns this, he must become a good gymnast and have good control of temperament.

---

[38] *Ibid.*, Ch. III.

Perhaps the discipline which is required is no better illustrated than by the teacher, who is one of the villagers. He said that after studying gymnastics for more than ten years, he had studied traditional Chinese medicine. Asked if he thought any of the craft might be lost, since it was passed from generation to generation without the aid of a textbook, he replied: "When a teacher gets old, he passes on all his craft to his pupils without reservation. Whether or not they learn depends on their individual efforts and intelligence." It is commonly understood within the community that nobody is qualified to teach until his own teacher authorizes him. In addition to this informal norm, there is also the more formal Government requirement that a teacher must have a licence and pay a tax. It is entirely possible that a teacher may have formal recognition but may not be recognized by the community.

New members are usually introduced to the cult by other pupils or inquire because of its reputation. The fact that the cult does not actively proselytize is explained by the teacher: "We do not advertise or propagandize since our forerunners did not." He emphasized that there is no screening process or admission requirements:

It's unnecessary because the bad ones would not dare to come. It is hard work and it is very difficult to complete training within a short period of time. Without humility and patience one cannot get anywhere.

At the time our observers were in the resettlement area there were between twenty and thirty people (both male and female and including several individuals who were from outside the resettlement area) actively involved in learning the traditional arts. Each of these pupils paid a monthly fee of fifteen dollars. Occasionally, the *qi lin* dance team is asked to perform in the downtown area. For their services they receive approximately two hundred dollars an hour. According to the teacher they also "voluntarily provide their programme in the resettlement area when there are festivities during the year to please the Gods."

The layout of the flat in which cultic activity takes place is similar to those around it. On the door to the flat are three pieces of coloured paper: red, yellow and green. These pieces of paper are *fu* 符, or charms which are to prevent evil influences from entering the "temple." One charm is illustrated below.

```
Seat of the

Holy Mother

Incantation Order

to Drive Out

Evil Spirits

and to Invite

Blessings Back

to the Hall
```

Opposite the door in the main room where the lessons are given is the altar area, and hanging on the walls around the room are framed congratulatory notes sent by friends when the gymnasium opened. To the far left of the door is a shelf on which the head of the *qi lin* is kept. Chairs and drums are stored underneath. Near the door there is a phonograph which is used by the students of the school during leisure hours.

The altar area on the far side of the room contains red shrines or God shelves. The shelf of the local Earth God rests on the floor of the flat and is approximately three-fourths the size of the larger one dedicated to the founder of the cult, which hangs on the wall. Each of the shrines has three lamps and a tablet behind it. "Temple of Bamboo Wood" is written on the tablet in the upper shrine. The tablet for the Earth God is framed and inscribed, "A full house of gold and jade." A couplet below reads: "The vanguard and dear patron Gods of Riches; the five sides and five Earth Gods of Dragon."

When a pupil enters the gymnasium, he pays respect to the tablets of the Grand Teacher (the founder) and the Earth God. He bows in front of the tablets and places lighted incense sticks on the two shrines. The students avoid placing the same number of incense sticks on each altar, in deference to the Grand Teacher, since it is customary to place more sticks of incense on his shrine. Usually, pupils use three sticks of incense, placing two on the shrine of the Grand Teacher and one on the shrine of the Earth God. Asked why one should place unequal numbers of incense sticks on the shrines and why it is necessary to bow three times, one of the pupils said, "I don't know; this is merely our tradition."

The lessons usually begin by practising the system of movements of the *qi lin* dance. Often the teacher beats the drum himself. At the drummer's left a man strikes a gong; the cymbalist is at his right. During practice exercises, advanced pupils teach the less advanced, the teacher supervises and the dancers change several times in order to allow everyone to participate. Then the pupils perform another set of movements, often the brandishing of a club and sword followed by traditional Chinese boxing.

The teacher of the Mantis Health Centre combines the activities of the gymnasium with the practice of Chinese medicine. He said he has qualified as a teacher and herbalist only within the last two years. As a result, when he first opened the school people were skeptical of his competence until he had cured several patients. He specializes in fractures, bruises, external wounds, rheumatism and other trauma. Apparently there is little doubt about his ability to heal. One of the resettled villagers remarked: "There are several who have broken either arms or legs and who have been cured by him. My own hand (he showed his right hand) was badly broken but he treated it and with one set of medicine I was cured."

Asked about the kind of medicine he uses, one informant said, "Mostly grasses, tree roots, etc. However, his remedy for fractures and bruises is refined from the rust of iron." When asked to explain the medicinal use of iron rust, he replied: "He is able to make medicine from rust. In fact, the more rust the better. After the rust has been refined it is soaked in medical wine and made ready for service."

Apparently his business has developed well; one informant said that many people go to him. Asked how much he charges, an informant said, "Eight dollars for a prescription for people who come from his village. Others are charged fourteen dollars while some have to pay as much as twenty dollars."

GHOSTS

An understanding of the Chinese idea of *gui* or ghost requires a prior understanding of the nature of man in relation to cosmic reality.

Earlier in this chapter we explained that traditional Chinese cosmology rests upon the concept of the general animation of the whole universe and that this animation has both a positive and a negative aspect; that is, it is both *yang* and *yin*. A living man has within himself both positive and negative forces. He has both the *san hun* 三魂 (three spiritual energies) and the *qi po* 七魄 (seven emotions).[39] Physical death results in a separation of these *hun* and *po*. To this explanation must be added the idea that the deceased depend upon their relatives for the maintenance of their existence. Such existence may be ensured by proper offerings and worship by appropriate male descendants. If the deceased are not properly provided for, their *gui* or ghosts appear. Since they partake of the *yin* element they are usually evil. Their condition is wretched indeed, for they have no place where they belong. As Werner points out, they are denied both reincarnation on the one hand and eternal bliss on the other.[40] Eventually, they cease to exist, but before they do they can cause a great deal of trouble. The *gui* of someone who has died an unnatural death may return and seek revenge. This belief is illustrated by two comments of the resettled villagers.

> There is no doubt about the existence of ghosts. Following the riots last year, almost every day someone was killed by a motor car near a well-known restaurant in Kowloon. This makes clear the existence of the ghosts of the wronged . . .

> These are bad things; the ghosts of the wronged never take rest.[41]

Many of the Plover Cove villagers believe in ghosts. A village elder tells how he encountered them during the Japanese occupation. He was walking home one night when of necessity he passed by the spot where not long before a number of persons had been executed. He was horrified when he heard a loud wailing sound coming from the place of execution and saw shadowy forms which he identified as the *gui* of the departed ones. Later, an inscription was set on a stone to mark the exact place where the ghosts had been seen to warn passers-by of the possible danger there. These ghost inscriptions are seen in many rural areas.

---

[39] Werner, p. 417.

[40] *Ibid.*, p. 231.

[41] This restaurant is thought to be operated by persons of leftist political persuasion. Leftist violence during the disturbances of 1967 was responsible for the deaths of several people.

In spite of how one feels, it is best, upon meeting a ghost, to show as much bravery as possible. One informant said that to refrain from wiping perspiration from one's forehead when walking at night indicates that he is not afraid of ghosts. One young man is said to have whipped a ghost with a rope and lived to tell about it; another scared a ghost away by simply whistling.

Ghosts often carry out their evil intentions by attaching themselves to a person causing him to become sick or insane, or even to die.[42] At such times it is helpful to burn mock coins and paper money in order to persuade the ghost to leave. Sometimes a qualified person is called into the sick room to write a charm which is attached to a wall or the ceiling. The magic of the charm may succeed in exorcizing the evil spirit. Ghosts are worshipped and exorcized whenever necessary, but especially during the seventh month when they are believed to be unusually active.[43]

Once, in the resettlement area, a woman attempted to recall the soul of her grandson. Apparently, some of the older people believe that when a child is sick his soul leaves him because he has been frightened by someone or something. If the child is to recover one

---

[42] For an early description of this belief, see N.B. Dennys, *The Folk-Lore of China* (London: Trübner, 1876), Ch. VII.

[43] See Bronislaw Malinowski, *Magic, Science and Religion* (New York: Doubleday, 1948). Malinowski discusses the efficacy and *raison d'étre* behind acts of magic. Magic is a part of any act of entreaty to supernatural forces or beings (albeit with a considerable element of coercion), in response to situations when "Man, engaged in a series of practical activities, comes to a gap" (p. 79). By "gap" he means any strange, mysterious and therefore feared phenomena for which there are no sure techniques of control. A mingling of strong desire, anxiety and fear, and the sense of confrontation with a greater unknown force *(Mana, waken)* is the essence of the act of magic, or of any religious belief. Man may desire to control, but his actions are based on beliefs grounded in "the sublime folly of hope." "Folly" here is used deliberately, as Malinowski suggests that primitive man no less than the most sophisticated theologian grapples with the mystery and awe of the unknown (p. 90):

> Looking from far and above, from our high places of safety in developed civilization, it is easy to see all the crudity and irrelevance of magic. But without its power and guidance, early man could not have mastered his practical difficulties as he has done, nor could man have advanced to the higher stages of culture. Hence the universal occurrance of magic in primitive societies and its enormous sway. Hence do we find magic an invariable adjunct of all important activities. I think we must see in it the embodiment of the sublime folly of hope, which has yet been the best school of man's character.

must call back his soul and ask him not to be afraid. An observer reported the following:

> The woman ran to the playground. There she faced the east, and waving the child's coat over three sticks of burning incense, she sang in a moaning voice, "Sister, be good; sister, come back! Grandmother will take sister back! Don't be afraid! Sister, would you come back and get better day by day?" She carried on like this for about ten minutes. Afterwards, she walked back to her flat. Shortly, I deliberately walked near her flat and heard her still crying upstairs, "Sister is frightened by the two four-eyed girls! Oh, don't be afraid!"[44]

According to some of the resettled villagers, the child's coat would then be used as a pillow for the child to sleep on that night. Apparently this rite is usually performed by the child's grandmother or in her absence, by the mother. Men do not take part in this rite and it seems to be confined to older people.

There is some evidence that belief in the power of ghosts is declining. One informant said: "I am not convinced of the power of ghosts. I take it that evil cannot win over the right. And after all, ghosts are the spirits of men." Another informant said that very few, if any, ghosts had been seen since the move to Tai Po. Asked why he thought this was so, he said he didn't think ghosts would like to come into Tai Po, for they prefer dark places and the streets of Tai Po are well lighted at night.

PERIODIC WORSHIP

In the foregoing sections, we have considered the various supernatural beings worshipped by the Plover Cove villagers. We now turn to a brief description of the various forms of related periodic worship.

The Chinese calendar is a lunisolar one in which the cycle of the moon determines the months of the year. The moon symbolizes the great *yin* force in the universe as over against the sun, which

---

44 The observer later noted that the Hakka term translated "sister" here means "child" and may be either male or female. The observer thought the reference to the two four-eyed girls was to the two American social scientists who wore glasses and who were living in the same apartment as our observers. In all fairness to the "two four-eyed girls," it should be noted that there was an influenza epidemic at the time.

symbolizes the *yang*. Asked for evidence of the importance of the moon as related to life, one villager pointed out the effect of the changes of the moon on the tides. It follows quite naturally that the times at which the moon begins to wax and wane are understood as especially significant. Apparently the phases of the moon demonstrate the *yin* principle, which in its relationship of duality with the *yang* principle constitutes the fundamental reality of life and indeed, sustains the universe. The tradition of periodic worship on the first and fifteenth days of the month has developed accordingly.

This worship is most commonly observed at the altars and shrines in homes and places of work. The shrines are usually made of wood and painted red and may honour any of the household or traditional deities described earlier. They are found in a variety of different locations. Some are hung on an inside or outside wall; others may be placed on the ground near the doorway; still others may be found inside a home or shop along the floor, against the wall or in a corner. The size of the shrine and the elaborateness of its fittings vary widely. Usually a red electric lamp, consisting simply of a light bulb, is installed in front of the shrine. There may be more than one lamp. An observer, after reporting on a number of shrines each with one lamp, went on to describe a shrine with three lamps.

> This one had three lamps, one in the centre, one on the right and one on the left. The lamps were all red; the ones at the sides were bigger than the one in the centre. I entered the shop and asked the man why there were three lamps in his shrine while others had only one. He said that in his shrine the small lamp in the centre belongs to the Gods while the other two belong to the shrine.

Some persons allow the lamp to burn continually; others turn it on just in the daytime; still others light it on the first and fifteenth days of the month. There seem to be no hard and fast rules governing these practices, and reasons given for variations seem to have nothing to do with belief systems. An observer reported on one man's comment regarding his lamp, which burned continually.

> I asked again why the lamp at the altar should be lit every day. Mr. Wong replied that there isn't a switch for the lamp. Furthermore, the small red lamp uses little electricity and so they leave it on day and night. As a matter of fact, it would be quite sufficient to light it just on the first and fifteenth days of the lunar month.

In addition to red lamps, most shrines are fitted with holders for burning incense and candles, which may be burnt on any day but usually only on the first and fifteenth days. On these days, one first cleans the shrine and then burns incense, once in the morning before going to work and once in the evening between dinner and bath time. The worshipper stands before the shrine, holding before him three sticks of burning incense. He then either simply bows three times, or if he wishes to show special reverence, he goes through the ritual known as the Three Kneelings and Nine Kowtows, kneeling three times and kowtowing three times each time he kneels. He then places the incense in the holder. The worshipper is more often a woman than a man or a child. Sometimes food is offered along with the incense, although monthly periodic worship seems usually not to include food offerings; they may be an addition at unusual times when special thanks are to be expressed or supplications made.

The great range of accepted practices and attitudes regarding periodic worship indicates that this aspect of the life of the Plover Cove people, like most other aspects, is undergoing change. There are people who try as strictly as possible to carry on traditional practices, which on the first and fifteenth days include not only worship at home but also visits to temples and abstinence from meat.[45] An informant said:

> There are, of course, pious people who abstain from eating animal flesh on the first and fifteenth days in the month according to the lunar calendar and who also go to the temples to pay respect to their Gods.

In contrast to such persons, who seem to be in the minority, there are many who have installed shrines in their homes and shops but leave them unattended even at the designated times for periodic worship. One observer reported that on the first and fifteenth days, some shops had their shrine lamps burning and some did not; some had incense burning and some did not. One woman, in a conversation with another on the fifteenth day, casually remarked that she had simply forgotten to burn incense. On another occasion, an observer, after visiting a home, gave this report:

> In the front part of the sitting room there was a little shrine made of wood and painted red. On top of the shrine was a tiny red electric bulb to replace the red candle. The bulb had not been

---

45 This form of abstinence could be the result of Buddhist influences.

lit, and so I inquired, "Today is the fifteenth day of the month; why don't you put on the light?" His answer was really unbelievable, for he said, "They say that this can save electricity." I was in great doubt and asked, "Is it really for the sake of saving electricity?" He assured me that this was quite true.

The villagers continue to believe in a variety of supernatural beings and related forms of worship. Although some Gods were left behind, many have been carried into the new environment. Worship usually takes place at home but may also occur in a temple, an ancestral hall or at some special location such as a grave, shrine or object of unique spiritual significance. Rituals and ceremonies vary both in nature and in meaning. People worship during major festivals, on special days associated with individual deities such as the birthday of Tian Hou (twenty-third day of the third month) and the birthday of Guan Yin (nineteenth day of the second month), at times of special importance for individual or family and periodically on the first and fifteenth days of the month.

CHRISTIAN MISSIONARY EFFORTS

Christianity seems to have had very little influence on the resettled villagers. Only one person among the villagers known to us seems actually to have been converted to Christianity. This girl says that she was converted after reading a biblical tract.[46] The fact that she seems to be a social outcast may have been one cause of her conversion or may have resulted from it. Several of the children of the resettled villagers are going to church supported schools, but they seem interested only in education. Although in some schools periods of religious instruction are compulsory and there is considerable peer group pressure to participate in them, these attempts at gaining the students' acceptance of Christianity have not been successful.

There are Christian symbols displayed rather prominently in at least two flats of the former villagers. Interestingly enough, both of these flats belong to people who left the villages as young men and went abroad to work. Their return coincides closely with the removal.[47] One gentleman has a large picture of the birth of Jesus

---

[46] We have reason to doubt that her conversion was a direct result of reading a tract. However, this is the generally accepted story in the resettlement area.

[47] Apparently, many men who were overseas at the time when the move was announced returned to get their share of the compensation.

hanging on the wall of his sitting room directly above a God shelf for traditional Chinese deities. Asked about this apparent contradiction, he explained that while he was abroad he was converted to Catholicism, but since his return to Hong Kong he has begun once more to practise traditional forms of worship. His attitude provides an illustration of the eclectic nature of Chinese religion as discussed in Chapter I.[48] The other flat has a crucifix hanging in the living room. The owner lived most of his life in a nearby country, married there and raised his children. His children were converted to Roman Catholicism in the schools, and their belief is the apparent reason for the cross on the wall. This gentleman claimed that he does not believe in any god. There were no other religious symbols in his flat. He said he did not feel any social pressure from the other resettled villagers as a consequence of his children's Roman Catholicism.

The staff of a sect-related mission centre in the resettlement area is actively engaged in proselytizing. There are also people representing other groups who come in from the outside. The efforts of these people seem to both amuse and annoy the resettled villagers. One method used by the mission centre staff is to walk through the resettlement area while one person plays an accordion and others pass out tracts and invite people to meetings. For the most part, the resettled villagers do not appreciate this procedure. One young man responded to being handed a tract by saying, "What use is this? I never read them; I just throw them away." If the rest of the young respond in this way, the audience for tracts is extremely limited because most older people, especially the women, are illiterate.

Another technique is to hold a slide show and invite children by broadcasting over a public address system. Slides of wild animals and beautiful landscapes are shown, and as a centre worker put it, "We connect them with the gospel message, Bible teaching and stories." The slide show is usually in two parts separated by preaching. On different occasions, slides of interest to adults are shown and related to the gospel message.

---

48 Theoretically, this gentleman's actions might be explained by in-group norms. It seems apparent that he responded to the social pressures both overseas and at home. The classic discussion can be found in William F. Whyte, *Street Corner Society* (Chicago: University of Chicago Press, 1960), pp. 3-104, esp. pp. 94-104. In less technical terms, "When in Rome, do as the Romans do" seems to fit.

On several occasions, our observers noted that the centre was nearly full for such meetings. However, close checking among the resettled villagers revealed that Plover Cove people were not attending. One young man who had attended a few of the meetings summed up the situation in this way: "Thoughts about Jesus just aren't good listening. Nobody from the six villages believes. The believers are the people who rent our flats and who come from other places." Aside from a status problem, we do not know why this should be true. We do know that the resettled villagers, unlike some of their tenants, do not go to the centre to get the occasional distributions of rice and relief goods. It seems that the mission centre has nothing which is very attractive to offer the villagers.

Many of the resettled villagers are openly hostile toward attempts to convert them. One reacted to evangelists in this manner:

> They were here a little while ago, but nobody could understand what they were talking about. We ignored them and they soon left us alone. People are always coming to preach to us, but I wonder why we should believe in their religion.

Some of the people reported that when the evangelists came to see them they simply told them, "Go, don't play the ghost!" Apparently they feared the evangelists, like the *gui*, would bring evil influences.

To a group of people who are very pragmatic about their religion, and who have in the past adjusted their religious beliefs to meet the needs of their situation, conversion to Christianity seems not to make a great deal of sense. A woman expressed it quite eloquently:

> We Hakkas do not believe in Jesus. Those who believe in Jesus are beyond us. What have those people gained from believing in Jesus? All they have been given is a little grain. Someone told us that our soul would go to heaven if we believed in Jesus. How do we know things after death?

Belief in Christianity seems to present the resettled villagers with a status problem. The social distance between the former villagers and the staff of the mission centre seems to be so great that the villagers feel uncomfortable in the presence of the centre workers. Therefore, the villagers tend to avoid interaction with them as much as possible. This social distance is a product of the superior educational level of the centre staff as well as their relative sense of sophistication about the urban environment, a sense which the former villagers are still acquiring.

Finally, it seems that the resettled villagers see Christianity as confusing and complex, in contrast to their own religion which they find simple. An observer asked one man whether Christianity could not be considered simpler because you only had to worship one God instead of several Gods. He replied, "I don't burn incense or light candles; who said it is not as simple as yours?"

SUMMARY

The impact of the new urban environment is resulting in changes both in the villagers' belief in supernatural beings and in related worship. One woman summed it up by saying that her people do not take their worship of Gods seriously any more. This statement is certainly not true as a generalization. It does, however, point to the impact of the new environment on the old religion, which has produced a very wide variety of attitudes and practices. It is significant that there is so little expressed resistance to change, and that such a high degree of tolerance for lack of uniformity can be sustained.

This highly individualistic approach to religious practice seems to have sources in the complete lack of theological beliefs of these villagers, and also the inability of older villagers (who held power through wealth and prestige in the villages and tend towards religious orthodoxy) to enforce uniformity now that the villagers are dispersed and their behaviour is not so visible to the other villagers. This breakdown of traditionalism in ritual practices, however, may not herald the complete decline of all traditional religious practices. The villagers, allowed to choose what to each individual seems a "comfortable" religion, are likely eventually to have a highly egocentric religion based upon each individual's private concerns and emotional needs. What will survive will probably be scattered and partial representations of the total tradition. But a religion with such great elasticity and adaptability to individual preference need not be either accepted or rejected as a totality. Accordingly, the survival of at least remnants of the religious tradition seems highly probable.

Chapter V

RITES DE PASSAGE

Birth, Marriage and Death

INTRODUCTION

Every person in human societies is expected to perform certain duties and in turn is granted certain rights, because of the positions he fills. In the resettlement area it is commonly accepted that older children should care for younger ones. It is not unusual to see ten or twelve-year-old girls carrying their baby sisters or brothers on their backs. This is a duty of children but not, for instance, of young married men. Similarly, young children enjoy the right to play and to engage in certain activities while the same behaviour on the part of the young married man or older child would be frowned upon by the community.

When we use the term "status" we are imputing to it a dual significance. Status may mean "a position in a particular pattern"— for instance, in a family, a bureaucracy or a community—in which case an individual may hold positions in several patterns (or "institutions," as we used the term in Chapter I); thus we may speak of the "statuses" of a person. It is also possible to refer to an individual's collective statuses as his "status."[1] Linton points out that there are two types of statuses, ascribed and achieved. Accordingly, he says ascribed statuses are those assigned without reference to ability. One example would be those rights and duties assigned to all individuals in a community because they have in common a certain age or sex. Achieved statuses are those positions which may be earned because they have qualitative requirements.[2] A person's status or position changes as he moves from one category of ascribed status to another or qualifies for movement from one achieved status to another.

---

[1] Ralph Linton, *The Study of Man* (New York: Appleton-Century Crofts, 1963), p. 113.

[2] *Ibid.*, p. 115.

When discussing status it is impossible to avoid a discussion of the term "role" because role and status are inseparable. Linton defines role as "the dynamic aspect of status," or the behaviour expected of occupiers of certain statuses.[3] In other words, role is the performance of status prescriptions.

At this point it is appropriate to ask: by what mechanism does an individual learn his roles? Newcomb gives some insight into the socialization process when he suggests that everyday roles are matters of response to the anticipated behaviour patterns of others. He points out that children practice the roles of others in society in such a way that interaction involves either playing various roles themselves or alternating roles with other children. The importance of this role playing is that the child is responding to the behaviour of others and indeed is able to play the role of others. Newcomb concludes that people acquire knowledge of norms and roles by responding to the anticipated behaviour of others whom they view as dependable.[4] George Herbert Mead calls this response "taking the role of the other."[5]

Van Gennep has said, "An individual life, whatever the type of society, consists in passing successively from one age to another, and from one occupation to another."[6] In other words, an individual life consists of passing from one status group to another, and the passage from one status group to another is facilitated by anticipatory socialization. For example, as a young person develops he begins to accept the values and orientations of the group in which he does not yet hold membership. Similarly, he begins gradually to share fewer and fewer of the values and orientations of the group in which he has membership. Merton, in a discussion and reformulation of the data of Stouffer, *et al.* in *The American Soldier,* has pointed out that movement between status groups is expedited by the individual's anticipation of membership in the non-member group and the attendant acceptance of the values of that group.[7]

---

3 *Ibid.,* p. 114.

4 Theodore Newcomb, *Social Psychology* (New York: Dryden Press, 1950), pp. 305-308.

5 George H. Mead, *Mind, Self, and Society,* ed. C. W. Morris (Chicago: University of Chicago Press, 1934), Part III.

6 Arnold van Gennep as cited in William J. Goode, *Religion Among the Primitives* (Glencoe, Illinois: Free Press, 1951), p. 183.

7 Robert K. Merton, *Social Theory and Social Structure* (New York: Free Press, 1957), Ch. VIII, esp. pp. 265-271.

This anticipation of movement between status groups may result in a marginal situation for the individual in which he finds himself accepted by neither group.[8] It is at least to these crises of transformation that men in every society apply their religious beliefs. The rituals associated with the various crises have become known as *rites de passage*.[9]

Ritual is considered by some scholars to be the medium of expression for those experiences which cannot be communicated in any other way. It arises out of an urgent need to communicate without adequate understanding of the reasons for that need. It is only later that rationalized purpose becomes attached to the ritual act.[10] In one sense then, the *rites de passage* inform the wider community of an individual's change of status. These rituals pinpoint the time of passage, insuring that every individual in a society has a clear-cut ascribed status.

However, *rites de passage* are more than a method of communication. Ritual provides a concrete symbolization of attitudes; that is, it objectifies attitudes: constant rehearsal of ritual reinforces the attitudes so symbolized. The observance of ritual and the reminder of the attitudes objectified therein serve to reinforce group solidarity. As Parsons put it,

> For by the common ritual expression of their attitudes men not only manifest them but they, in turn, reinforce the attitudes. Ritual brings the attitudes into a heightened state of self-consciousness which greatly strengthens them, and through them strengthens in turn the moral community.[11]

---

8 Our use of the term "marginal" refers to a person's suspension between status groups. The original usage of the term referred to a person suspended between two cultural groups, not fully identified with either. Robert Park, the originator of the concept, used it with reference to people of mixed blood, as well as more generally of those individuals who owe allegiance to two cultures, being fully accepted by neither. See Robert E. Park, *Race and Culture* (Glencoe, Illinois: Free Press, 1950), pp. 345-392.

9 Joachim Wach, *Types of Religious Experience, Christian and Non-Christian* (Chicago: University of Chicago Press, 1952), p. 42.

10 Susanne K. Langer, *Philosophy in a New Key* (Cambridge, Massachusetts: Harvard University Press, 1957), p. 40.

11 Talcott Parsons, *The Structure of Social Action*, 2nd ed. (Glencoe, Illinois: Free Press, 1949), p. 435. The same idea is expressed in Emile Durkheim, "On Communal Ritual," trans. Joseph W. Swain (1954), in *Theories of Society*, ed. Talcott Parsons, *et al.* (Glencoe, Illinois: Free Press, 1961), pp. 959-960.

BIRTH AND CHILDHOOD

The participant-observers engaged in this research project were able to identify several age-graded status groups among the inhabitants of the resettlement area. The most clearly defined were observed among the young. Only vague distinctions, with the exception of the elderly, appeared among those twenty or more years of age. The youngest status group is that of children who are called "baby"; they are between one and five years of age. Boys in this category can be readily identified because they wear only a shirt and no pants. From six to ten a youngster is called a "child," and boys wear short pants. Up to the age of ten, children seem to be relatively free of responsibility. At eleven, children become responsible for light work such as sweeping, cooking and caring for younger children, and a boy begins to wear long pants. The term "young people" identifies this status group. At approximately sixteen, the young person becomes a "young adult" and is expected to engage in an adult occupation. At this age, young people begin to attend religious festivities. The badges which distinguish a young adult are clothing of improved quality, rings and watches. The girls' movements between status groups are not so apparent as the boys'. For instance, clothing does not change since the girl wears a coloured print shan ku 衫褲 from babyhood until her marriage when she adopts the customary black or dark blue shan ku.[12]

None of the transitions between these status groups involves very much ritual. For the resettled villagers ritualistic practices play a significant role in marriage, death, birth and to a lesser extent, in the two important birthdays, the twenty-first and the sixty-first.[13]

---

12 The shan ku is the traditional dress for village women. To the Westerner, it resembles a pair of fitted pajamas. This type of dress is worn throughout the year, supplemented with warmer layers in the winter. The trousers are loosely fitted for the younger women and become even looser as age increases. The top piece has a tight mandarin collar and clasps across the chest under the arm; the sleeves may be short or long. The top fits down over the waist, and there are pockets on the inside where money and valuables can be safely kept.

13 The Chinese consider an infant to be one year old when he is born. A person's age changes on New Year's Day although the celebration of Chinese birthdays falls on the seventh day after the lunar New Year (called "everybody's birthday"). If a child is born shortly before the New Year, he is two years old, in the traditional Chinese way of thinking, when he may be only a few days old by Western calculation. Therefore the twenty-first and sixty-first birthdays take place at approximately age twenty and sixty for most Chinese.

Childbirth was certainly one of the crises in village life. A combination of two factors was involved in the situation: the importance of continuing the line and the high mortality rate for both mothers and infants. The Chinese attach great importance to having an heir, especially a male heir, to venerate them after death.

The unsanitary conditions in the village and the lack of competent and knowledgeable people to provide medical services resulted in sizable death-rates among infants and mothers, both at time of birth and thereafter. The mother-in-law customarily attended the expectant mother, or in her absence, a "professional" midwife was hired. This woman's sole qualification was some experience delivering babies. One informant summed up the situation: "Because of the inconvenience of transport it was nearly impossible to take the expectant mother downtown and the outdated method of midwifery carried with it painful risks with a high death-rate for both mothers and children." The perils of the situation are illustrated by the fact that the celebration of a child's birth was delayed until one month after birth, probably to assure that the baby was going to survive. One informant, a school teacher who lived in the village for some years, estimated the infant mortality rate in Plover Cove at fifty percent. However, other informants, mostly village representatives, estimated infant mortality at twenty-five percent. This latter estimate is probably more nearly accurate and is comparable to estimates of twenty-eight to thirty-three percent in two other village studies.[14]

In the villages, the religious ritual associated with childbirth followed a fairly standard pattern. Three days after the baby was born the family shared chicken cooked in ginger wine with the neighbouring families, especially the old women.[15] If their economic situation allowed, they repeated this celebration on the seventh and twelfth day after birth. This observance announced to the community that the baby was in good health and that everybody was happy. On the nineteenth day after the birth it was customary in Plover Cove, especially if this was a first-born child, for the maternal grandmother to prepare a meal using five or six chickens, biscuits made from herbal grasses intended to drive away the evil spirits, different kinds

---

14 Fei Hsaio Tung, *Peasant Life in China* (London: Routledge and Kegan Paul, 1939), p. 33; and Martin C. Yang, *A Chinese Village* (London: Kegan Paul, Trench, Trübner, 1948), p. 11.

15 The description of a similar observance is to be found in Yang, p. 128.

of homemade cakes, steamed pork with a sauce made of cured beans, lotus seeds, nuts and other good foods.[16] If the baby was a boy, the occasion warranted more of everything. Since removal these customs have not been so elaborately celebrated. Certainly some of the afore-mentioned items, particularly herbs, are not so readily available in the resettlement area. Even if they were, the cost in herb shops is often prohibitive. In the village economy these items were usually gathered by women in the hills.

Traditionally the most important observance of a child's birth has been the *man yue* 滿月 (one month) celebration. The customs on this occasion vary. Fei reports the belief in "spirit sadism" where the child is shaved and given a personal name, usually one of abuse, by the maternal uncle in the hope that the child will not attract evil spirits.[17] Burkhardt describes the occasion as a festive introduction of the child to the world and as an occasion when the child is taken by the mother to the local temple in order that she may invoke the protection of the Gods for the child.[18] For the resettled Plover Cove villagers a feast seems to be the most important aspect of the *man yue* celebration. In the village period the feast was held in the courtyard but now the villagers go to a nearby restaurant. One informant said a recent *man yue* party required ten tables in a local restaurant.[19] Sociologically, the feast functions to promote group solidarity. These people do not seem to attach much religious significance to the occasion. We have no information which indicates that they visit local temples (such as that of Ma Niang) or their own ancestral halls on this occasion. As we shall see in regard to the marriage rite, convenience may be an important factor.

In the villages there were no printing facilities and invitations were passed by word of mouth. However, since resettlement, it is con-sidered fashionable and proper to send written invitations on such occasions. One informant explained that word-of-mouth invitations are no longer adequate because one does not know whether the

---

16 *Ibid.*, p. 125. Yang observed that in Taitou the child's maternal grandmother brought presents and congratulations to the child's family.

17 Fei, p. 35.

18 V. R. Burkhardt, *Chinese Creeds and Customs* (Hong Kong: South China Morning Post, 1955), II, 150-151.

19 The Chinese figure meals in terms of tables. At a feast ten to twelve people usually sit at one table; for a good meal, the cost starts at approximately $150 per table. Consequently, ten tables would cost about $1,500.

invitation is sincere. Only if you receive a written invitation do you know that you are being shown respect, that you are considered a true friend. Having received the written invitation, you then attend the function. This state of affairs is interesting, since many of the villagers cannot read.

MARRIAGE

In discussing the functions of traditional Chinese religion, Yang notes that the significance of ancestor worship attendant to the marriage rite is securing the ancestral temple for the predecessors and assuring the continuity of the line.[20] In the resettlement area ancestor worship is no longer a part of most marriage ceremonies. Thus, these functions of ancestor worship in the marriage rite have ceased to exist for this group of people.

We can, however, document among the resettled villagers the religious element of predetermination.[21] The continuation of such traditions as the selection of correct dates for marriages and the reliance upon matchmakers provides a way of cushioning emotional disappointment in case of an unsatisfactory marriage. Instead of blaming the failure on traditional wisdom one blames it on fate. Needless to say, this orientation enhances the possibility of social integration within the family because it focuses possible conflicts outside this institution.

At least three additional functions of the marriage rite for the family can be suggested. First, the marriage rite indicates a family's social status by exhibiting at least one component of social status, wealth, to the rest of the community. The elaborateness of the feast, the number of guests, the gifts and the size of the dowry all signify wealth. During a discussion of wedding gifts, one informant said:

> Generally speaking, when it comes time for a married woman's nephew to be married and she is poverty stricken, her parents may give their daughter money to buy a silk curtain in order for her to save face. This is because during the wedding feast relatives ask one another about the presents they sent. If her gift is a silk curtain she will not have an inferior feeling. When she returns home after the feast her brother would also thank her by giving her some money.

---

20 C. K. Yang, *Religion in Chinese Society* (Berkeley: University of California Press, 1967), p. 54.

21 *Ibid.*, pp. 55-56.

Showing off one's wealth is certainly involved in this example. The result of such a display of wealth is that the family reinforces its social status in the eyes of the community.[22]

Secondly, the marriage rite reinforces social stability by a ritual demonstration of the ideal roles and statuses of each member of the family. Thirdly, group solidarity is reinforced by delineating the in-group and the out-group. All of these functions are illustrated in the events following the wedding feast when relatives stay to tease the bride and groom. The bride is taught by her sisters-in-law how to address her relatives and is in effect having her new position in the well-known pattern of relationships reinforced. A by-product of these practices is that she becomes identified with the family and its internal relationships, no matter how unpleasant the process.

One of the informants in the resettlement area reported several Hakka sayings concerned with marriage. Some of the marginal crises can be identified from these sayings. For instance, "A girl takes a husband and a boy takes a wife." This saying indicates that the people conceptualize marriage as a definite change of status, a transition from being a boy or girl to being a responsible person in a unit relationship. "The girl leaves her home, then she belongs to her new home." This saying gives further indication of the change of status which takes place during marriage. The position and set of relationships which a girl had in her own family are not the position and the set of relationships she must assume within her new family. Both the boy's and the girl's statuses in the social structure are illustrated by the proverbs: "A girl is just a room for the boy but a boy is the whole house to a girl"; and "Females have no independent character; they have to obey their fathers at home, their husbands after marriage and their sons after their husbands' deaths." Social stability and social control are reinforced by such sayings as: "Marry once only" (applying to women); "Marriages are based on parents' commands and the matchmaker's words"; "Follow whoever you marry"; "Every happy marriage is pre-arranged."

The meagre subsistence of these villages (pointed out in Chapter II) and its effect on marriage rites are indicated by the number of marriages which took place after removal when financial resources

---

22 T. Veblen, *Theory of the Leisure Class* (New York: Modern Library, 1934), supplies the classic discussion of wealth and its use to display social status.

were available to contract marriages in a suitable manner. The out-of-proportion number of unmarried males in the village period further indicates the economic situation. It should be kept in mind that marriage was exogamous and that the financial expectations of the wife-supplying family made it hard for the villagers to find satisfactory mates. They were often unable to meet the demands.

Although we have no exact figures, it is apparent that this situation was partially ameliorated by the taking of child brides. This practice was common prior to World War II and has occurred since then, though less frequently. The system of child brides existed among the poor. It functioned to assure a bride to the groom and lifted the financial burden of raising the girl from her parents while providing an extra pair of hands for the boy's family. The little girl was usually purchased by the boy's parents just after she was weaned. She was expected to work for the groom's family, although she was not treated as part of the family. The villagers cited the frequently harsh treatment of child brides as one reason why the system fell into disuse. In the villages the highly unpredictable economy based on fishing and agriculture made an additional pair of working hands, even those of a child, or the absence of an additional non-productive person from the household (the work expected of a daughter being a great deal less than that expected of a child bride), could make the difference between starvation and minimal subsistence.

At about the time for the marriage ceremony, the girl was sometimes sent back to her parents. The usual rites of marriage were then performed. Apparently the contract was often broken prior to the actual marriage, if the bridegroom had a serious physical deformity. For the Chinese, social stigma attaches to physical deformity and assuring a wife for a deformed son was a non-economic reason for taking a child bride.

The actual reasons for the diminishing importance of the system of child brides are not at all clear. The villagers' concern about the harsh treatment often afforded the girl is less than convincing, since it does not explain why a sense of moral responsibility should prevail over economic hardship, although one respondent, herself a child bride, stated that she would have starved to death rather than expose her daughter to the experience. One suspects that the child bride system's diminishing use is the result of an attempt to bring practice into line with laws promulgated against it by the Government, and that moral concern and its use as justification were a result of the promulgation. The other possibility is that economic conditions in recent years have not been quite so severe.

We have noted that the villagers were exogamous. (See Chapter II.) Each village had a single surname, and marriage with anyone of one's own surname was considered improper. Within the Cove, there were five Lei villages and one Wong village. Since a Lei could not marry a Lei, the only possible combination within the Cove was a Lei-Wong marriage. Sheer numbers dictated that marriage had to be contracted with people living outside the Cove. But the limitations of numbers and the impossibility of marriage within the clan were not the only factors affecting whom one could marry. There were norms against marriage to people named Wan 溫 or Yip 葉 because most villagers believed that such liaisons would result in no offspring.

From what we can gather, the engagement of couples in the village occasionally took place as early as the age of eleven or twelve, although most couples were engaged two years or less before their marriage. Because of the economic situation, marriages often took place so late that there were no offspring.[23] Finding an appropriate marriage partner for one's son or daughter was handled through a matchmaker, usually in the nearest market town, Tai Po. The engagement proceedings were controlled by the matchmaker and the remaining traditions of the three documents and the six formalities.[24] The parents had no idea who their future daughter or son-in-law was. Indeed, the tradition was that the couple should not meet one another until the day of the wedding, although there are indications that

---

23 This problem is still being solved for some people in the resettlement area by "purchasing a child." We understand that the price of a small boy is approximately $2,000. The Chinese do not frown upon this practice because it may solve the problem of too many children in the selling family and the problem of a male heir in the buying. In the long run the child may be much better off.

24 The three documents (san shu 三書) are the pin shu 聘書, which is the letter of willingness to fix the agreement to marry the girl signed by the boy's parents; the yun shu 允書, which is the girl's parents' reply that they are willing to give her to the young man; and the hun shu 婚書 which is the form of the agreement. The liu li 六禮 (the six formalities), are the giving of a goose (yan 雁), the giving of a piece of red silk (na cai 納米), the asking of the names of both sides (wen ming 問名), the acceptance of each other (na ji 納吉), deciding on the date (qing qi 請期) and the wedding (qin ying 親迎).

parents tried to get information from outside sources prior to the wedding. The matchmaker started by trying to interest both sets of parents in the prospects. When the parents were satisfied that there was potential for a satisfactory match, the birth dates of both the boy and girl were professionally calculated to see if they suited one another. The matchmaker then became the emissary between the two families for negotiating the amount of money that would change hands between the families contracting the marriage.

The *shen jia yin* 身嫁銀 often amounted to as much as $2,000, which in the village economy was a very sizable sum.[25] Some people were forced to sell land in order to raise the money. In economically depressed families where there were many sons, parents were deeply concerned about this matter. The *shen jia yin* was given to the bride's parents as a dowry to be spent for family dinners and in preparing things for the bride to take with her. The bride's parents were expected to contribute an amount equal to the *shen jia yin*. The amount of money spent was so important to the reputation and social status of the parents that they usually bargained very hard. Occasionally the bride's parents spent some of the money for something other than the impending marriage, but such action was frowned upon and caused great loss of face.

After the money problems had been negotiated, a fortune teller was consulted to choose a lucky day for the engagement.[26] On the day chosen the boy sent the girl an engagement ring through the matchmaker. At the same time the boy's parents sent some pork, two sterilized chickens and one-third to one-half of the *shen jia yin*. In turn, the girl's family wrote the exact hour and date of her birth on a piece of red paper and sent it with a pair of chickens, a hen and a cock, and a silver ring to the boy's family, using the matchmaker as intermediary. At the girl's home a few relatives were invited for a simple meal, but at the boy's home there was no special celebration.

---

[25] *Shen jia yin* means "money of marriage." The idea of marriage money seems to be closely related to the idea of bride price. For a discussion of bride price and its relationship to the family see Ruth Bunzel, "The Economic Organization of Primitive People" in *General Anthropology*, ed. Franz Boas (New York: Johnson Reprint Corporation, 1965), pp. 383-387.

[26] The Chinese almanac provided the necessary information for choosing an auspicious day. For further information see the discussion of the Chinese calendar and the related materials cited in footnotes three and four of Chapter III.

The matchmaker was given about $200 for services rendered. After the engagement day a few months or as much as two years were spent in preparation for the wedding and choosing a lucky day for it.

The traditional engagement practices of the villagers have undergone changes. Some of these changes are due to the transition between village life and the urban environment while others, often associated in the minds of the villagers with the transition, began prior to resettlement. The concept of *zi you lian ai* 自由戀愛 has become a common expression among the resettled villagers and simply means the Western pattern of courtship and marriage. The extent to which the young people in the resettlement area have adopted the new pattern of *zi you lian ai* is not at all clear. The evidence suggests that both patterns are now used. Nor is it clear to what extent traditional practices—such as the *shen jia yin,* the calculation of birthdays and the choosing of the lucky day—are incorporated into the new pattern. We do know that there are varying degrees of acceptance of the new pattern on the part of older generations, as illustrated by comments from two of the resettled villagers:

> The young no longer marry when their parents tell them to marry. Rather, they marry each other because they have a mutual understanding and they believe that life together will be happy. This is free, fair and reasonable.

> Matchmakers introduced my daughters. I am very strict with them. How can they arrange their marriages by themselves? The reputation of the family is most important. If they go astray I will chop them with knives!

Following the engagement and prior to the wedding there was considerable activity. Several informants told about Hakka terms which were related to this period. For instance, the term *kai jian* 開剪 (open scissors) indicates that the girl should spend a goodly portion of time preparing a wardrobe. It was especially important for girls to make their underwear after the wedding date was chosen. It may be that some girls continue this tradition, but in recent years girls seem to have been buying ready-made or tailored clothes. Three obvious reasons for such purchases are: ready-made clothes are available and inexpensive; the villagers' economic conditions are improved; and young girls' factory employment provides more money to buy clothes and less time to make them.

Another term, *kai mian* 開面 (open face), refers to a young girl's changed hair style signifying her engagement. Apparently this hair style still announces that its wearer is no longer available for marriage.

According to custom, during the village period, an engaged girl wove several *hua dai* 花帶 (literally, flower ribbons). We have been told by informants that the meaning of this was "silk ribbon as long as heaven" or "long life, being rich, noble and lucky." These ribbons were about two feet long; the bride gave them to other unmarried girls prior to the wedding and to maidens in the boy's home after marriage.

Apparently some of these ribbons were given away at an occasion known as Bao Ri 報日. Twenty days before the wedding the boy's family sent a card to the girl's family along with a pot of yellow wine, a pot of white wine, thirty *jin* 斤 of bean curd, thirty *jin* of pork and some water flour.[27] The girl's family used these gifts to invite the village people to a feast at which the bride gave the flower ribbons as gifts. The resettled villagers did not mention nor did the observers note the practice of these latter two customs in the resettlement area. Nevertheless they may still be practised, at least occasionally.

During the village period it was the engaged young man's responsibility to make ready the furniture which would be needed for the new home. Just as ready-made clothes are now bought and for the same reasons, furniture is no longer made by hand but is purchased in a shop. Furniture in Hong Kong, especially that imported from China, is very inexpensive. Thus making it by hand would hardly be practical, even if the resettlement premises made carpentry feasible.

With the Chinese emphasis on the family and the continuation of the lineage, much importance was attached to the assembling of the bed. Prior to the wedding, (on an auspicious day chosen by a fortune teller), two *hao ming po* 好命婆 (fortunate women) undertook the assembly of the bed pieces.[28] While assembling the bed they were to recite four sentences:

---

27 A *jin* is a catty, about one and a third pounds.

28 A fortunate woman was usually between fifty and sixty years of age with a husband still living and many children and grandchildren.

It is good to assemble the pieces of the bed on a lucky day.
The bed must be made ready to welcome the bride.
A hundred sons and a thousand grandsons come from the bed.
May the husband and wife live till they are white-haired and have
many years.

We strongly suspect that, like many other practices, this one was left behind in the village.

The wedding day was and still is a festive, but also physically and emotionally exhausting, occasion for the bride and groom. In the village period, preparation by the boy's family on the wedding day, including decorating the sedan chair, often began as early as one o'clock in the morning. During the morning there was a ceremony for bestowing a flower and a red ribbon on the groom by the elders of the village. Preferably, the elders involved in this ceremony were wealthy and had children and grandchildren. While bestowing the flower and red ribbon they were to recite four sentences:

Holding hat in hand finish placing on it the silver flowers.
Bestow the hat—rich, noble, glorious and elegant—on top of the
head.
Bestow the famous flowers plus the red ribbon which attires your
body like a yellow dragon,
Wishing that you as husband and wife live together until white-
haired and that you have the good fortune to become a civil
and military hero.

The elders involved were rewarded for their contribution with a red *li shi* packet. When the preparations were completed and it came time, as the villagers would say, to go to the girl's home to welcome her, a procession was formed with the sedan chair carried by professional chair carriers hired for the occasion. The bridegroom, with uncles and brothers, accompanied the chair part way and then returned home. The rest of the procession continued to the girl's home. Well-to-do families in the villages employed a Chinese band and performers to accompany the procession. When the procession reached the bride's home and the bride had ascended the chair, the return trip to the boy's home began, the performers doing the *qi lin* dance, the band playing and the rest of the group setting off firecrackers, all guiding the bride to her new home.

Some of our informants seemed to lament the fact that in the resettlement area the procession, which must have been both colourful and noisy, no longer occurs. Since removal, the automobile has replaced the sedan chair, as it probably would have done earlier if cars could have reached the villages. According to the villagers the result of introducing the automobile has been the end of the Chinese band and the unicorn dance in the wedding ceremony. There may be other reasons as well for this change. Elsewhere in Hong Kong, wedding cars are frequently observed to be followed by a nine-seater van carrying a Chinese band. The bridal car is usually a relatively new car decorated with a bridal doll, curiously enough with Western features and dress, mounted on the hood with ribbons running back to the front doors. A Government ban has eliminated the use of firecrackers.

In the village when the bridal chair reached the boy's home its door was placed in the direction which had been divined from the Gods prior to the ceremony. After the chair had been placed in the appropriate direction two *hao ming po* helped the bride out. The two women held a bamboo sieve covered with a pair of the bridegrooms trousers over the bride's head and showed her into the house. As the bride entered the front door of the house, she should by tradition step over a *li tou* 犂頭 (coulter of a plow heated red hot),[29] to insure that she brought no bad elements to the groom's family. While the bride was dismounting from the chair and entering the house, the bridegroom was supposed to keep himself hidden. An encounter before the bride first entered the house was considered unlucky for the couple. After the bride had entered the house the feast began; it was usually held in the open court in front of the house under a canvas cover.

Some of the people in the resettlement area have retained some of the customs connected with entering the house while others have

---

29 This custom has been dropped because, as one villager put it: "There were so many complicated and trivial customs which gradually got left out." Apparently heating the coulter red hot was too much of a problem. This was without doubt a purification rite. For the bride who had previously been married it was necessary to step over the burning reins of the type used to guide the water buffalo. For further discussion of purification rites in other societies, see Roger Caillois, *Man and the Sacred*, trans. Meyer Barash (Glencoe, Illinois: Free Press, 1959), pp. 139-151 (Appendix I entitled, "Sex and the Sacred; Sexual Purification Rites among the Thonga"); and Paul Friedrich, "Semantic Structure and Social Structure: An Instance from Russian" in *Explorations in Cultural Anthropology*, ed. Ward H. Goodenough (New York: McGraw Hill, 1964), p. 137. See also Mircea Eliade, *The Sacred and the Profane, The Nature of Religion*, trans. Willard R. Trask (New York: Harper and Row, 1961), pp. 77-78. Eliade suggests that the purification rite annuls the past and that it actually abolishes past time.

abandoned them. Feasts are no longer held in the courtyard in front of the house because there are none in the resettlement area.

Because the resettled villagers now hold feasts in restaurants, changes in guest lists and other arrangements have become necessary. In the village an invitation to the festivities was sent to all close relatives and to a minimum of one representative from each village family. Frequently invitations reciprocated those previously received from other families. A gift, usually money, was the necessary response to an invitation. The villagers kept account of what was given by different individuals and when it came time to respond with a gift, an equal amount was returned. Another factor determining the amount was the closeness of relationship. Money thus received was used to defray the expenses of the feast. In the village the usual amount was two to five dollars; now the proper gift is ten dollars. On the other hand, it is now standard practice to invite only one person from a family.

Instead of a monetary gift, it was possible to give the couple a tapestry or silk curtain. Material for dress-making was placed between two sticks of bamboo. The character for happiness, xi 喜, was embroidered on gold paper in the middle of the cloth with the name of the receiver in the upper right-hand corner and the name of the sender in the lower left-hand corner. There was no uniform cost for tapestries; some cost as little as ten dollars while others might be several times that. Occasionally, rich people ostentatiously pinned bank notes to the tapestry. This kind of gift is still possible.

The bride's paying of respect to the groom's ancestors was perhaps the most important part of the wedding festivity in the villages. According to our village informants this ceremony usually took place during the feast. It was conducted by an elder who welcomed back the Gods by placing incense and a portion of rice on the luo ge 羅格 (a box for gift articles) and intoning a welcome to the Gods. After the bride had paid her respect and the feast had ended, the elder sent the Gods back to their places. One informant explained that choosing a lucky day was necessary partly in order to bring back the Gods, who will appear only at certain hours of certain days.

As we investigated whether this practice has been carried over into the resettlement area we discovered that, like many others, it was not followed extensively even in the village. One informant had a charming story for explaining that ancestor worship did not take place in the wedding ceremonies in his village:

> Once an elder who was to officiate at the ceremony for calling the Gods during a wedding was late because he had been smoking opium. The guests became impatient with the long wait and the leader of the village, sensing their irritation, got up and declared in public: "The ceremony of inviting back the Gods is henceforth forbidden. Continuation of this kind of ceremony will result in our having no offspring at all." Since that time the tradition of inviting the Gods at weddings has disappeared, but it survived in some other villages.

There is no reason to doubt that an incident like this actually happened. However, a much more plausible reason for the decline of this custom is that it was physically inconvenient. This village, as well as three of the others in this study, had no temples. Indeed, in order to pay respects to one's ancestors, one had to make a journey of considerable distance over difficult paths. Interrupting the marriage feast to make such a journey was not practical. A relevant point to be kept in mind is that these Hakka do not usually keep ancestral tablets in their homes; there is no real alternative to temple worship. At the present time, the former residents of Chung Pui, which is the only village having a temple in the resettlement area, would find it convenient to continue this practice.

After the feast the other guests left, but the relatives stayed to tease the newly-weds. The bride was not allowed to sit, and maidens from the groom's family taught her how to address all the bridegroom's relatives. Often this activity continued until the early morning hours. This particular tradition has been continued in the resettlement area.

On the morning after the ceremony the bride was expected to get up to work before everyone else in the household and to go to bed only after everyone else in the evening. It was her responsibility to take good care of her parents-in-law, serve them tea and prepare their bath water. The new daughter-in-law was supposed to obey her mother-in-law. The birth of the first child marked the daughter-in-law's true entrance into the family.[30] Up to that time the couple was supposed to be very reserved before parents and others.

The whole idea of the subservience of the bride to her mother-in-law seems to be breaking down. Earlier we noted that the Western

---

30 Fei, pp. 46-47.

concept of courtship and marriage is becoming common among young people. Further, it is worth noting that the introduction of *zi you lian ai* into the tight kinship system is forcing a change in relationships. It has been observed in other studies that traditionally in a conflict situation between mother and daughter-in-law, the son, at least in the early days of the marriage, sides with the mother.[31]   However, if the young people's choice of their own partners is based upon affection, the son tends to support his bride.   Additionally, the contract is between the young and not, as in the past, between their parents; this change may introduce tension between the bride and her parents-in-law over their respective roles.   Previously, relationships were well-defined and were closely linked to the way in which marriages were contracted. Many of the women in the resettlement area are concerned about this problem.   One of them commented, "Formerly daughters-in-law were absolutely obedient but now they have more freedom.   Sometimes mothers-in-law have to tolerate them even if they have a fiery temperament."

DEATH

The occurrence of death in any society creates an emotional and social crisis for family and friends.   Normally the death of a single individual does not affect the whole society unless that person is extremely important or powerful.   For the family in which a death occurs, not only are emotional attachments severed, but relationships and responsibilities must also be realigned to cover the gaps caused by the death.   The marginal crisis in the situation is not that of the individual who dies but of those who survive and find themselves in a new social situation.   Here again, ritual expressions soften the impact of the situation by providing a means of expressing emotion and group solidarity.   It has been suggested that among the Chinese the rituals strengthen the individual's orientation toward the family.[32]

In the villages the family notified friends and relatives of a death by distributing mourning notes.   Such notes were usually written on white foolscap size paper and stated the deceased's name, age, sex and time of death.   The name of each son, daughter, daughter-in-law and grandchild was written on a red piece of paper approximately two inches wide which was pasted onto the white mourning note.

---

31 *Ibid.,* pp. 47-48.
32 Yang, *Religion* . . . , p. 35.

In addition to informing neighbours, friends and relatives, close relatives were also responsible for preparing the body for burial. Relatives of the same sex as the deceased cleaned and dressed the corpse and laid it in the coffin. In the village the coffin was placed in the courtyard outside the house. In the resettlement area, of course, there are no such courtyards.

After receiving a mourning note, friends and relatives were expected to respond by preparing gifts for the mourning family. The gifts—sometimes pork, chicken and other foods, but most often money or cloth, called *zu bu* 族布 ("clan cloth")—were used to pay respect to the deceased. Each individual took his gift to the coffin and paid homage to the deceased, leaving the gift on a table.

The villagers do not completely agree as to the nature of the funeral rites. Some said that it was not necessary to invite monks to be in charge of the burial. However, at a recent funeral for one of the resettled villagers, the family invited some monks to sing and read scriptures during the evening preceding the funeral and until the next morning. One villager maintained that they should have a *gong de* 功德 service.[33] In this matter, as in many others, the depressed economic conditions in the villages prevented the people from inviting monks. In the case of this recent funeral the son-in-law, who was living with his mother-in-law at the time of her death and who himself is not a villager, may have had different traditions. The incident serves to illustrate how varied the traditions may be even within one small community.[34]

The basic ceremony seems to be the paying of respect by the survivors: children, daughters-in-law and grandchildren. All of them kneel beside the coffin. The children and daughters-in-law wear white coarse hemp clothes over regular wearing apparel and white shoes and hold a *xiao xiang gun* 孝相棍, a piece of bamboo about a foot in length with one end wrapped in red cloth. While in the kneeling position there is general wailing, especially from the women. The grandchildren wear similar white cotton mourning clothes and white shoes and kneel but need not hold the *xiao xiang gun*. The burial, which usually takes place on the second day, follows the paying of respect by other relatives.

---

[33] Kenneth Scott Latourette, *The Chinese: Their History and Culture* (New York: MacMillan, 1964), p. 538. Latourette notes that Buddhist and Taoist monks might be called in to chant from their sacred books to help the soul of the deceased through possible sufferings.

[34] This matrilocal residence is itself highly unusual and points up again the relative wealth of the villagers since resettlement.

In the village, burial was preceded by a procession from the house of the deceased to the grave. Approximately ten people, all relatives from the same village, "carried" the coffin, some actually bearing the weight and others simply holding its edge. A comparatively rich family sometimes employed a band to accompany the procession. The coffin was preceded by relatives holding bamboo sticks with zu bu suspended from them much as a flag is carried. At the grave site it was customary for the mourning family to give a handkerchief and a white envelope containing twenty cents to each person attending. When the deceased had been buried the mourners took off their mourning clothes and dismantled the zu bu as the zu bu might be used later for making clothes.

The resettlement area, the urban environment surrounding it and the new economic status in which the villagers have found themselves have allowed and forced the resettled villagers to adjust their burial practices. The coffin is no longer carried in a funeral procession but is taken in a hearse-like vehicle with a flower arrangement around a picture of the deceased displayed on the top. Workers are hired to carry the coffin. Interestingly enough, villagers are still buried in Plover Cove.

After the burial there is a period of mourning, the length of which varies in different situations. Informants in the resettlement area tell us that the duration of the mourning period depends not only upon the economic situation of the family, but also upon such other pressing commitments of its younger members as regular jobs and school work. We were told that in the past a mourning period of at least one hundred days was considered appropriate, but more recently mourning has continued for from seven to forty-nine days.[35] In some cases the mourning period varies according to the sex of the mourner, women mourning an odd number and men an even number of days.[36]

---

[35] At least one other author has noted a mourning period of forty-nine days or alternatively a number of days which is an odd multiple of the number seven. See Burkhardt, III, 80.

[36] Contrast footnote number 30. Apparently this particular custom is related to the principles of yin and yang. The yin is the female principle and is associated with even numbers while the yang is the male principle and is associated with odd numbers. According to these principles, it would seem our villagers have reversed the custom. A possible alternative explanation (and one which has a parallel in Chinese medicine where one takes a yin medicine for a yang illness and vice versa) is that females, in order to compensate for themselves as part of the yin principle, mourn an odd number of days or in accord with the yang principle. Similarly, men

Arriving home from the burial, the family constructs a moon-gazing house of bamboo for the soul of the deceased. This house is kept indoors. For the first week after the burial respect is paid before it both morning and evening by placing candles, wine and the leg of a pig in front of the house and sounding a gong so that the soul knows that worship is taking place. During the first week the same pig's leg can be used every time, though it is supposed to be heated before each use. After the first week worship is held once every seven days.[37]

Children, daughters-in-law and grandchildren must attend the weekly worship even if they live inconveniently far away. The mourners pin a small piece of black cloth on the sleeve, the left sleeve if the deceased was male and the right if she was female. During the mourning period the males should not have their hair cut and no one in the family should attend celebrations. They are permitted, however, to go to work.

When the head of the family considers that the time has come to terminate the period of mourning, he uses red paper to write a note to every member of the family. He should also make new clothes for each member of the family and prepare food and wine for the occasion. At seven o'clock in the evening on the appointed day all members of the family pay respect before the moon-gazing house. The mourners burn paper images of items—furniture, money, boats—which they think the ghost will need in heaven. They also burn their mourning garments and put on the new clothes. It is appropriate for friends and relatives to send a whole roast pig for worship purposes. After the ceremonies, all the mourners sit down for a meal. Usually the host prepares a white pig for those who helped at the funeral service.

The cost of the funeral varies considerably with the economic situation of the family. The recent funeral in the resettlement area cost approximately $10,000. One informant itemized the approximate expenses as being $1,000 for the monks who performed the *gong de* service, $700 for the coffin and $1,100 for the flower car; the remaining $7,200 was spent for feasts and such other expenses as the

---

would compensate by mourning in accord with the *yin* principle. We cannot verify which, if either, of these interpretations is the correct one because the villagers cannot explain why they follow this custom. For a short discussion of *yin* and *yang*, see Samuel Couling, *Encyclopaedia Sinica* (Shanghai: Kelly and Walsh, 1917), p. 615.

37 Burkhardt, p. 80.

moon-gazing house. Although we do not know the cost of this particular moon-gazing house, we are told that these houses might cost anywhere from one hundred to several hundred dollars. One informant said that even the poorest family must spend approximately $1,000 for a small funeral. Such a small amount of money would not allow for many mourners.

At present, the villagers are better able to afford the costs of a funeral than when they lived in Plover Cove. Rural people devise ways of meeting such expenses. For example, the Union of the Rural Committees has an association for the elderly called the Fu De Hui 福德會, a welfare club. When a member of the Hui dies, each of the living members contributes some money, usually fifty cents. This money, which often totals several hundred dollars, is then turned over to the family of the deceased, enabling them to provide adequate burial rites.

So far our discussion has been concerned with religious observances at the death of adults. Yang observed that in Taitou the elaborateness of the funeral was conditioned upon the economic situation, the age of the deceased and the number of surviving generations.[38] Examination of grave sites and *jin ta* 金塔 (gold towers) would indicate that this is also true of the Plover Cove villagers, the placement and size of the graves of children and young people being relatively less significant. Although we were not able to observe the funerals of younger people and children in the resettlement area, there is no reason to think that the customs established in the village have changed. However, it may be that all funerals have become relatively more elaborate with the increase in prosperity.

---

[38] Yang, *A Chinese Village*, p. 89.

Chapter VI

ANCESTOR WORSHIP AND RELATED PRACTICES

ANCESTOR WORSHIP

The fact that ancestor worship has pervaded so many life situations and crises is ample evidence of its importance in Chinese life and religion. Latourette says, "No other phase of Chinese religious life was more prominent than the ceremonies for the departed. They constituted, indeed, one of the outstanding characteristics of Chinese culture and were an integral part of that most potent of Chinese social institutions, the family."[1]

The origins of ancestor worship are vague. Some scholars feel there is substantial evidence that many ancient traditions from which ancestor worship stems were reinterpreted by Confucius and his followers.[2] Certainly temples and ceremonies honouring the ancestors existed prior to the time of Confucius.[3] Fitzgerald contends that in ancient feudal times ancestor worship was the cult of the noble clans and that the peasants (who were actually serfs) did not participate in the veneration of ancestors. In fact, he says that during this era the peasants did not even concern themselves with who their ancestors were. He argues that the earliest ancestor worship was really a fertility cult, citing as evidence palaeographic studies indicating that originally the character for ancestor was a phallic symbol.[4] Whether one accepts Fitzgerald's arguments or, for that matter, any of the many others about the origins of ancestor worship, it seems clear that it is not entirely a Confucian development. Still, although the influences of Buddhism, Taoism, animism and other practices of religious

---

1 Kenneth Scott Latourette, *The Chinese: Their History and Culture* (New York: MacMillan, 1964), p. 537.

2 C. P. Fitzgerald, *China*, 3rd ed. (London: Cresset Press, 1961), p. 45; and D. C. Graham, *Folk Religion in Southwest China* (Washington, D. C.: Smithsonian Press, 1961), pp. 45-48.

3 Latourette, p. 536.

4 Fitzgerald, pp. 45-50. At one time the character for ancestor 祖 was written without the radical as 且. This has been found rendered on oracle bones and bronzes as 且 which Fitzgerald considers a recognizable representation of a phallus.

significance are discernible, one has finally to admit that a large proportion of the ceremonies and concepts are Confucian.[5]

In its purest Confucian form, the emphasis was on paying respect to the values of the departed. However, Graham notes that in folk religion the emphasis seems to be on worshipping ancestors as deities.[6] The Chinese have historically viewed making sacrifices to the ancestors as of the utmost importance in order to secure the blessings and the protection of the spirits. Apparently any tendency to neglect them or to perform the rituals improperly was thought to bring about misfortune.[7] Fitzgerald has related the neglect of ancestral spirits to the *gui* discussed in Chapter IV:

> It is the fear of this last and irremediable catastrophe, the extermination of the clan, and the transformation of the ancestral spirits into miserable ghosts, which was, and still to the mass of the Chinese people is, the chief incentive to continue the male line, the profound cause for which male children are esteemed above all

---

5 Latourette, p. 537.

6 In Graham's words (p. 120):

A very important question is, Do the Chinese worship their deceased ancestors as gods, or merely honor and respect them as men? Addison, in his excellent booklet "Chinese Ancestor Worship," asserts that the Chinese do not worship the deceased ancestors as deities (Addison, 1925, p. 52), but honor them as noble and exalted human beings. This I have found to be the belief and attitude of most of the more intelligent and enlightened Chinese in West China. For years, I inquired about ancestor worship only from the more educated Chinese, and always received the same reply—the ancestors after death are human beings, highly respected, but not worshipped as gods.

One day I was talking to a servant, a Chinese who had no schooling and who was steeped in the popular ideas and beliefs of West China. I asked this man, "Do the Chinese worship their deceased ancestors as gods?" He replied, "Yes, We common Chinese have a proverb, *'Ho ti shih jen, shih liao shih shen.'*" This means, "Living they are people, after death they are gods." Later the writer put the question to many other common Chinese people of West China and always received a similar answer. Scholars have also agreed that the common, uneducated Chinese of West China worship their deceased ancestors as gods, while reaffirming that the more enlightened Chinese do not.

The reference in this quotation is to J. T. Addison, *Chinese Ancestor Worship* (Shanghai: Church Literature Committee of the Chung Hua Sheng Kung Hui, 1925).

7 *Sources of Chinese Tradition,* ed. Wm. Theodore de Bary (New York: Columbia University Press, 1966), p. 7.

other blessings. They not only continue the living line, but, through the ancestral sacrifices which they alone can perform, they are indispensable to the continued repose and happiness of the ancestral spirits.[8]

Whether or not this fear is a motivating force for those among the resettled Plover Cove villagers who practise ancestor worship is hard to tell. We can document the fact that since resettlement some couples have been concerned enough about the lack of a male child to purchase a son. (See footnote 23 in Chapter V.) But whether these couples were motivated by a desire to continue the line or to have someone to perform the ancestral sacrifices or simply because a son is socially desirable cannot be determined. A combination of the first and third considerations may motivate some of the villagers who do not worship their ancestors.

Latourette suggests that it is not only out of fear of dire consequences that ancestor worship has been maintained over the years. For some, the continuance of the traditions may well express a genuine respect and affection for the departed. For others, ancestor worship may represent a desire to conform within the society or to win respect or influence in the eyes of neighbours.[9] That at least some of the resettled villagers do so desire is indicated by one young man's comment concerning the Chong Yang Festival: "Last year we went mid-way and turned back, which was a long-distance act." Making a pretense of going to the graves saves him from incurring the social disapproval of the rest of the community. Unlike the devout Buddhist who might make the attempt in order to gain merit, this young man was probably motivated mostly by the desire to maintain social relationships.

Another function of ancestor worship is the reinforcement of group solidarity. Yang describes great gatherings when all of the clansmen came back to pay respect to their common ancestors.[10] One can hardly deny that a large gathering and a sumptuous feast has psychological impact. For the resettled villagers, the gatherings have never been, nor are they likely ever to be, as grand as the ones Yang described. We noted in Chapter III that before resettlement the villagers who travelled to Wu Kau Tang did so as a group and that they did share a meal there. This custom has been continued in the

---

8 Fitzgerald, p. 44.

9 Latourette, p. 537.

10 C. K. Yang, *Religion in Chinese Society* (Berkeley: University of California Press, 1967), p. 43.

resettlement area. The trips to the ancestral hall and graves will continue to reinforce clan solidarity among the resettled villagers even if they survive only as social rather than religious occasions. If they disappear completely, an important prop of that solidarity will disappear with them.

Ancestor worship has also been regarded as a conservator of the past, as a moral and social control and as a check on individualism. Many of the young people among the resettled villagers seem unconcerned about the past or its tradition. Some are like the girl who went with her mother to worship only because it was expected. When asked to describe or explain certain religious practices she was unable to do so. How much of a moral force ancestor worship will be in the new urban environment with its competing moralities is hard to say.

Village ancestor worship was described in Chapter III in relation to the Field Festival. The extent to which it is practised in the resettlement area varies with village and age. There are four clearly recognized times for practising ancestor worship: the New Year, Qing Ming, the Field Festival and Chong Yang. Among the Chung Pui villagers, who have their ancestral hall in the resettlement area, nearly all the families worship on these days, according to the report of the *ci tang* 祠堂 (village ancestral temple) caretaker. In at least two instances families were represented only by one person. In one case the duties fell to the woman in the household. The village elder who had the key to the *ci tang* said nobody worships in the temple on the first and the fifteenth of the month: "Although today is the fifteenth day of the month, it makes no difference. Nobody worships in the ancestral hall on this day. Most people just burn some incense at home." We discovered, however, that the other villagers' record was not nearly so good. A visit to the *jin ta ci* 金塔祠 (the place where burial urns are stored temporarily) shortly after Qing Ming revealed signs of worship at only a few of the sites. From the comments of the resettled villagers we gather that ancestor worship is conditioned by convenience rather than necessity.

THE ANCESTRAL TEMPLES

It is not surprising that such an important religious practice should find expression in the erection and architecture of buildings. Ancestor worship is focused in the ancestral temple, which, as indicated in Chapter II, often occupied a central position in traditional villages.

Yang describes the ancestral temple:

> It was usually the largest and most impressive building of the whole clan. Its many halls and courtyards, its clusters of spirit tablets, and its imposing pillars and architectural decorations stood as a lofty symbol of the religious devotion of the clan to the spiritual values of the departed ancestors. In south China, where the clan was more developed than elsewhere in China, the size and elaborateness of the ancestral temple represented the wealth, influence, and distinction of the clan.[11]

While this description may characterize the modal case in China, it certainly does not describe the ancestral halls of the Plover Cove villagers. Of the six villages in the Cove, only two had ancestral halls. Some of the other villages are said to have had branch temples, but the evidence indicates that while these temples may have had spirit tablets for the Bo Gong, they definitely did not have ancestral tablets. With the exception of the two villages, the ancestral temples were located at Wu Kau Tang, and the villagers went there to worship their ancestors on the various important occasions during the year.

A trip to Wu Kau Tang revealed that the village temples located there are certainly not the grand structures one would envision from Yang's description. The appearance of these temples engenders doubt that they provide for the villagers a symbol of religious devotion to the values of departed ancestors. Indeed, the conclusion one might draw is just the opposite: that paying respect to one's ancestors is not of very great importance, at least for some of the villagers. One of the village temples is in a state of complete disrepair: the back half has collapsed and now has neither walls nor a roof. Another temple to which one of the villages is related is in what has been described as "less than prosperous condition." The other three are in better condition.

If it is true that the ancestral halls serve to display the wealth and influence of the villages, one could understand the disarray of these temples as a result of poor economic conditions in the villages. However, since removal there have been sufficient funds for maintenance and repair. Personal possessions seem to have displaced the ancestral hall as a means of displaying wealth. Certainly the resettled villager who has the latest in electrical appliances including an automatic washing machine, which he proudly displays in his front room, exhibits tendencies toward materialism. It may well be that the reluctance of some of the villagers to have the ancestral halls moved from Wu Kau

---

[11] *Ibid.*, pp. 40-41.

Tang to the nearby store fronts is related to the knowledge that the temples would then have to be kept in repair for people to see. The maintenance would cost money which, if spent in other ways, might bring more satisfaction.

The relocation of the temples at the time of removal and the subsequent problems make an interesting, if not instructive, story. In negotiating with the Government over the terms of resettlement, four of the villages applied for temple space in the resettlement area. The other two villages, the two which actually had temples in Plover Cove, attempted to persuade the Government to let them move their temples elsewhere in the New Territories. Finally, five of the villages were granted spaces for their ancestral halls in the resettlement area. The sixth village, the lone holdout, was granted permission to move its temple elsewhere.

Of the five villages which were granted space in the resettlement area, only one village installed its spirit tablet. The remaining four villages decorated the spaces as temples but never opened them. We found some evidence that there was never any intention of opening them, but that the spaces were sought from Government with the intention of turning them into money earning ventures. Asked, "Is that the ancestral temple of your village?" one older man explained:

> This is a model only. As we have just mentioned, the ground floors get higher rent so all of the villages applied to the Government for a ground floor flat to use as a *ci tang*. This was a lie. Inside these *ci tang* there is nothing at all and so the doors are kept closed all the time. However, among the five Lei villages, one ancestral temple is being used.

One village representative said that when he suggested that the temple for his village be moved to the resettlement area in order to make the ancestral hall more accessible to the elderly for worship, his suggestion was rejected by the villagers who cited *feng shui* (discussed later in this chapter) reasons which would bring bad luck. One suspects that one of the real motives was that the rather strenuous trip to Wu Kau Tang provided an excuse for not going to the ancestral temple very often and in the case of the elderly, an excuse for not going at all. It should be pointed out that even in the villages they did not go often, and some people did not go at all.

Recently the four villages have rented out their temple spaces to be used as factories. Renting out these spaces caused considerable contention among the people of one village. The particular village involved split along generational lines: the younger men (the women participated indirectly, if at all) argued that the temple space should not be rented out because they feared that the Government might not approve; the old men held that the temple space had been sitting idle long enough and it was time that it was rented. One old man stated the argument in this way: "Since the ancestral temple is not genuine it is a waste to let it sit vacant. It is for this reason that the elders of the village have been intending to rent it out for some time." Apparently the temples were not entirely unused; one young man commented concerning the temple of his village:

> The temple is useless. There are no gods in the *ci tang* but it is used for parties on occasion. Parties have been held in the ancestral temple many times, and there have been no complaints from the older people. The parties are usually limited to school-mates and friends.

The dispute was a simple power struggle between the generations. The older men had gone ahead with plans to rent the premises without first consulting the younger men. Since rental involved village affairs, and especially village income, the young men felt that they should be consulted; when they were not their social power was threatened. The young men made their point but eventually conceded, and the temples were rented.

Unlike the temple with clusters of spirit tablets described by Yang, temples in our study followed the Hakka custom of housing but one spirit tablet. Even before resettlement, the four villages which went to Wu Kau Tang to worship had no local tablets to their village founders. Each of the four traced its lineage back to Wu Kau Tang and kept and worshipped the tablet to its founder there. In an interview at Wu Kau Tang, a villager explained the situation:

> Q. Which temple is the largest in this area?
>
> A. The ancestral temple that belongs to Wang Leng Tau.
>
> Q. Does it belong only to Wang Leng Tau?
>
> A. No, it belongs to Wang Leng Tau and Chung Mei. The inside is very beautiful.
>
> Q. If it belongs to two villages, it must have two spirit tablets.
>
> A. No, it has only one.

Q. How do the people worship?

A. They kneel and burn incense.

Q. Do they worship the same spirit tablet?

A. Yes, with no differences.

Q. Is there any Chung Pui temple here?

A. No.

We have noted before that the Hakka people do not keep tablets for their ancestors in their homes, although they may have tablets to the local Earth Gods.

The one genuine ancestral hall in the resettlement area probably exemplifies fairly well the nature of the temples. In a large rectangular room, at the end opposite the door, is an altar with numerous incense holders. The wall behind it has a drawing of a female phoenix on the left and one of a male phoenix on the right. In front of the altar are three tables of decreasing sizes on one of which are two vases of gold plastic flowers. On worship days offerings are placed on these tables. Wooden stools line the side walls near the entrance. To the right of the door is a burner for paper offerings. Outside, to the right of the door, is a holder for incense for the Door God. On worship days one can see incense burning and the ashes of burnt worship paper lying about on the ground.

FENG SHUI

Feng shui 風水, or the art of geomancy, addresses itself to the proper balance and harmony of elements in natural surroundings. Apart from such occasional major disruptions as the result of public work projects (roads, bridges, excavations), the continuing interest of most people in feng shui is centered on the location of grave sites and the placement of buildings. Particularly with respect to the burial of the dead, feng shui is interpreted as vital both to the well-being and peace of the departed and to the prosperity of descendants and clans. It is often difficult to separate a sincere attitude of reverence and a certain aesthetic sense of what is "right" from narrow self-centered interests, although it would seem that both aspects apply to most individuals, whether traditionally oriented or otherwise.

Depending on one's point of view, *feng shui* practices are relevant to anything from philosophy and aesthetics through social psychology to manipulation (and/or exploitation) of people's ignorance and misfortune. But there is no doubt that *feng shui* assumes importance in the attitudes and actions of individuals and groups (whole villages or village segments); it provides a set of concepts through which men orient themselves to their natural surroundings and identify their place in them. The analogy is one between physical and spiritual harmony. If man can locate himself physically in the material balance of the universe, then he can maximize the virtue inherent in such harmony, and material well-being, prosperity, "the good life" will naturally follow. There seem to be no assumptions of an opposition between things of man and things of nature, no tradition that things "man-made" encroach upon and deface nature, as in Western thought. Western writers on the subject are keen to stress the non-Western nature of *feng shui* concepts. Freedman expresses it this way:

> One may stand by the side of a Chinese friend and admire the view . . . One's own pleasure is aesthetic and in a sense "objective": the landscape is out there and one enjoys it. One's friend is reacting differently. His appreciation is cosmological. For him the viewer and the viewed are interacting, both being part of some greater system. The cosmos is Heaven, Earth and Man. Man is in it and of it. So that while my characteristic reaction to a landscape may be to say that I find it beautiful, my friend's may well be to remark that he feels content or comfortable . . . the ideal case making him feel relaxed and confident.[12]

Feng shui thus provides not only a set of principles for understanding natural phenomena but also a way of explaining the fortunes or misfortunes of those who have made their place in a given setting. Aijmer stresses that concepts in *feng shui* contribute to group consciousness of a commonly shared situation and goals:

> Feng-shui is a ritual language: a set of symbols and ways of combining these symbols into ritual statements. The feng-shui language is largely shared and understood by all Chinese and it provides an important instrument in Chinese society for a diffusion of local ideas into the larger society.[13]

---

[12] Maurice Freedman, *Chinese Lineage and Society: Fukien and Kwangtung* (University of London: Athlone Press, 1966), pp. 121-122.

[13] Goran Aijmer, "Being Caught by a Fishnet: On Fengshui in Southeastern China," *Journal of the Hong Kong Branch of the Royal Asiatic Society, VIII* (1968), 75.

The feeling associated with *feng shui,* an "immediate experience" of "how the site feels," can be experienced with more or less intensity; geomancers stress the difficulty and discipline necessary for having the "sense" of a good site.[14]   The full complexity and esoterics of the art have become the special province of these *feng shui xian sheng* 風水先生   (*feng shui* professors) over centuries of practice.   In Freedman's view, it is vagueness combined with complexity and highly specialized technique that have kept *feng shui* beliefs invulnerable to skepticism and doubt, and held the curiosity and attention of gentlemen.   In fact, the practice is pursued with the greatest seriousness among the wealthy, and geomancers can and do command a high price as long as there are those in the society with wealth to spare and interests to protect.[15]   But *feng shui* beliefs endure among the poorest and most unsophisticated village people as well, and are practised within the limited sensitivity and ability of "laymen," or lesser geomancers, when the professional fee cannot be spared.[16]

---

[14] Andrew L. March, "An Appreciation of Chinese Geomancy," *Journal of Asian Studies,* XXVII: 2 (February, 1968), 259.

[15] See Freedman, p. 124:

Feng-shui is not like most of the rest of Chinese religion; there is no reliance on the will of a deity; there are no gods to serve or placate [see his exception on p. 124n]; it is based on self-evident propositions; the principles which regulate the cosmos, however vaguely they may be formulated, are known to experts who, in the performance of their professional duties, operate with sure techniques . . . One [consequence of this view] is that geomancers are held in an esteem not shared by other religious practitioners. They are gentlemen and attract the curiosity of gentlemen. The second consequence is that faith in geomancy may well survive a change in religion. Many Chinese Christians in the New Territories believe in and act by it.

And not only New Territories Christians believe, it seems. Graham has an interesting anecdote on this subject (p. 43):

About the year 1917, a relative of a deacon of the Baptist Church of I-pin, Mr. Chao Lan-t'in, died and was buried by Mr. Chao in the burial ground of the church of which I was then pastor. It was later disclosed that Mr. Chao, contrary to the church customs, had secretly engaged a *fengshui* professor to choose a lucky spot, and at the burial to point the coffin in the right direction. After a discussion by the church executive committee, Mr. Chao was required to remove the dirt from the grave, slightly change the direction of the coffin, and again cover the coffin with dirt.

[16] Such was necessarily the case with the poor Plover Cove villagers. One old woman observed that at one time the services of the geomancer had been fairly cheap but prices had been rising because of the increasing scarcity of sites (her interpretation). Thus *feng shui* practices were dying, although the beliefs were still taken seriously. The old woman reported one thousand dollars as the pre-resettlement price of locating a site; one gentleman living in the resettlement area of Tai Po is known to

Disappointment in the result of *feng shui* practice can be blamed upon error in technique, changes in the setting (*feng shui* operates in cycles) or, more profoundly, the attempt to manipulate its effects rather than to discover them:

> In the cosy universe to which filial piety is the key, then, a distant Heaven rewards virtue by preparing, in its nearer aspect of Creator, sites to which the just are led seemingly by chance. The good man trusts Heaven like a father . . . and does not try to force the natural mechanism by which Heaven accomplishes its design. [17]

Nevertheless, *feng shui* is often explained as a set of techniques and symbols "that can be played upon to the benefit of the player." [18] Drawing the line between manipulation and pious striving is difficult — at least for the observer. The "truth" of *feng shui* rests, on the one hand, on a reverse logic in which causes are deduced and legitimized through effects, and on the other hand, on its traditionally recognized value for interpreting the great mystery of why some succeed while others go begging — prosperity being the logical outcome of hard effort: "There is an important residue which eludes our categories and requires us to think as if what we separately call the psychic, the social and the natural worlds have a mutual coherence not reducible to strict 'causality.' " [19]

---

have charged three thousand. Evidently a number of geomancers came from the mainland and their numbers have probably decreased. It is interesting to note that a geomancer lived among Gallin's Taiwan villagers, practising his art "for a small fee." Gallin classifies him in much the same way as other diviners and religious functionaries. See Bernard Gallin, *Hsin Hsing, Taiwan: A Chinese Village in Change* (Berkeley: University of California Press, 1966), p. 245. Perhaps similar individuals operated among the Plover Cove villagers. In recent years, faith in their ability may have waned as the number of potential sites decreased. In the resettlement area the informal practice of geomancy becomes even more unlikely and difficult, but with greater prosperity it is highly doubtful that the number of good sites will be exhausted.

[17] March, pp. 266-267.

[18] Aijmer, p. 75.

[19] March, p. 264. See also a brief discussion of *feng shui* particularly in an historical context in Joseph Needham, *Science and Civilization in China* (Cambridge, Massachusetts, 1956), II, 359-363. *Feng shui* is also considered a part of "proto-scientific" techniques and attitudes in traditional China as opposed to Western developments. See, e.g., Volume III of the above work, pp. 150-168.

At any rate, most villagers took seriously the central concern of maximizing good influences by whatever means were available.[20] With respect to burial rites, we have noted that the cost of hiring a geomancer interferred with villagers' attempts to place graves "properly." In answer to a question as to how much burial rites cost the villagers, one man replied: "This is hard to say. Rich people bury in a grand and expensive style. Although poor families try to simplify every rite, they have to spend at least $1,000." This amount would have to cover costs over the entire mourning period and would scarcely be sufficient for the additional cost of a geomancer. Nevertheless burial in accord with proper *feng shui* was still desirable in the villagers' minds, if a site could be located by more informal means or if a change for the better in family fortunes could provide the necessary funds.

One expedient for prolonging the possibility of a proper burial as well as indirectly avoiding the unpleasant necessity of dispensing with *feng shui* considerations was the practice of double burial, a custom characteristic of southeastern China and noted by Freedman.[21] Double burial ultimately works to the benefit of those who experience difficulty in choosing a satisfactory final resting place. The body is interred, hopefully in a good place, and after seven or eight years is exhumed. The process of exhumation is referred to as "gold digging," or "digging bones." The name accurately describes what takes place, and the practice can be interpreted as a part of one's care for his ancestors. Gold Digging Day usually falls on the first day of the eighth lunar month. One villager described the day as follows:

> If it rains on the first of the eighth month, we do it on the second of the ninth month or on Frost Day. We change the date because it is inconvenient to dig the graves on a rainy day and because we have to avoid any evil. If you ask somebody to dig, you have to spend $50 to $60. I dug my parents' gold [bones] with my wife, but we would not let our children go. The bones had been buried for seven or eight years so they had an unpleasant odour. We cleaned each bone with paper and dried each one under the sun.

---

20 Although one village representative maintained a detached view: "This is something which does exist when you believe in it, and which is really nothing if you don't believe," another villager followed the logic that if all Chinese were careful to occupy the best sites for wind and water, the country would be strong. But given the obvious poverty in many cases, the practice was not reliable. The apparently increasing skepticism and doubt may be an expression of alarm at the number of settlements spreading over the colony and the decrease in good land, rather than overt disbelief.

21 Freedman, pp. 118-121.

Then we put them into a gold tower as close to their original form
as possible. As for smaller bones, we just put them inside in any
pattern.

Evidently this task, although part of one's duty to his parents, is
so unpleasant that many prefer to hire someone to do the job.
Prices quoted range from as little as eight or ten dollars to fifty or
sixty dollars. In general the cost is not prohibitive, and probably many
of the villagers handle the situation in this way.

The cleaned bones are placed in a *jin ta,* an earthenware jar about
two feet tall with a narrow neck sometimes (but not always) sealed
with cement. These jars are then placed in a *jin ta ci* ("golden tower
pagoda"), a rectangular, semi-enclosed cement structure located on a
hill a short distance from the village. Evidently there were ten or
more of these pagodas located near Wang Leng Tau, some containing
as few as two or three urns and others as may as ten or more grouped
according to agnatic kinship.

The villagers considered the *jin ta ci* only a temporary resting place
for the urns — they were stored there to await the important second
burial. The final burial was frequently delayed or never took place.
Given a time lapse of several years, the *feng shui* of a particular
ancestor became a less pressing problem, especially for a family whose
fortunes had not increased to the extent that they could afford the
geomancer. Hardship in such cases was hardly a disaster that could
be traced to the effects of one particular grave. In such circumstances,
feng shui practices are probably activated again only with a definite rise
in prosperity.

In most cases, the *jin ta ci* was in fact the final resting place for
the departed's bones. Anyone hiking through the New Territories
can see these urns, "weathered until they crack and spill their irrelevant
bones on the ground."[22]

The geomancy of architectural arrangements, as of the location of
burial urns, is very much a public affair, requiring the supervision and
approval of village elders, and accounts for certain regular patterns in
the layout of villages in this area. For example, it is considered
extremely bad *feng shui* for a dwelling to face the door of the ancestral

---

22 *Ibid.,* p. 120.

temple, yet it is desirable for all houses to be within sight of its doors, each house door facing in the direction of the temple door. This pattern is discussed in Chapter II.

We also noted in Chapter II that arguments over the relationship of objects to their surroundings (*feng shui*) often concealed disputes based on other grounds. *Feng shui* gives great play to individual wishes and frustrations as well as being one aspect of attention to the environment. In addition to generating conflict, *feng shui* aids in solidifying groups — in cementing hopes for the future that encourage cooperative effort.[23] March calls this the self-fulfilling property of *feng shui*, a kind of pulling up by the boot-straps.[24]

It is hardly surprising that any major public works involving large movements of earth and excavation raise loud protests as a result of the disrupted *feng shui* of graves and villages. The Government policy has been negotiation, often resulting in financial compensation to cover the expense of locating new grave sites and removing to them. This relocation was necessary for a number of graves and *ci tang* in the soon-to-be-abandoned sites in Plover Cove. The Siu Kau and Chung Pui villagers wanted the funds to select their own places to relocate the ancestral halls. Siu Kau persisted, and the Government provided $3,000 for the selection of a new site and preparation for construction and $5,000 for a special ceremony of spiritualization (Kai

---

[23] Freedman points out *feng shui's* relation to conflict situations, particularly within lineages, and even more in multi-surname villages where the struggle for dominance (if not outright forcing out) is even greater (Freedman, pp. 10-11). With respect to the geomancy of graves, he suggests the outlet provided for narrower, competitive striving (pp. 141-142):

If we now oppose ancestor worship to this view of geomancy . . . we shall see that in worshipping their ancestors the Chinese are stressing harmony and unity instead of competition and individualism . . . The difference between the two halves of the cult of ancestors can be further stressed by saying that whereas in ancestor worship men are under the dominance of their dead fathers . . . so that a hierarchy of forebears imposes a restraint upon the relations between living descendants, in the geomancy of burial men liberate themselves from their ancestors to give themselves up to an anarchic pursuit of narrow self-interest.

[24] March, p. 264. Aijmer also seems to be suggesting *feng shui* as a way of accounting for the greater initiative displayed by the Big Stream villagers in taking advantage of economic opportunities outside the village. Good *feng shui* was both the result of and impetus to adaptation, while the relative apathy of the Plum Grove villagers could in part be a result of their preoccupation with the fishnet facing them in the opposite hills, hanging over them like a Damoclean sword.

Guang 開光) when the move was made. The *ci tang* was eventually relocated in Fanling. The Chung Pui villagers settled for a *ci tang* located in a ground floor shop in the resettlement area. One shop was also provided for each of the other four villages. We have explained above that these shops have now been rented out as factories.

Many Government officials look upon such activities as barely concealed efforts to increase compensation, but even a little examination of villagers' — and urban dwellers' — attitudes reveals how seriously the matter is taken. *Feng shui* has occasionally been given as the reason for the voluntary removal of entire villages.[25]

The *feng shui* practices of the Plover Cove villagers were, for the most part, of a "do-it-yourself" variety, and interpretations of *feng shui* probably expressed the common desire for improvement and attempted to account for long periods of difficulty and hardship. (The concept behind the word "luxuries" had to be explained in interviews with the villagers.) In the resettlement area itself, the only *feng shui* problem noted so far has been the concern of shopkeepers whose stores directly face the *ci tang*; here mirrors have been put up to deflect bad influences.

With the radical change and the across-the-board increase in prosperity, much of the old conflict has doubtless become irrelevant. It remains to be seen if *feng shui,* especially urban *feng shui,* will continue to clothe new conflicts that may arise if, in fact, conflict still needs to be so muted. The increased amount of available wealth could, in the long run, result in an increased demand for the geomancer's services, particularly for the location of graves. Some such development may already be taking place: if the fees reported above for professional geomantic services are at all accurate, they have increased sharply within a relatively short period.

---

25 See James Hayes, "Movement of Villages on Lantau Island for Fung Shui Reasons," *Journal of the Hong Kong Branch of the Royal Asiatic Society,* III (1963), pp. 43-44; and James Hayes, "Geomancy and the Village" in *Some Traditional Chinese Ideas and Conceptions in Hong Kong Social Life Today,* ed. Marjorie Topley (Hong Kong: The Hong Kong Branch of the Royal Asiatic Society, 1966), pp. 22-30. *Feng shui* was the reason most commonly given by Plover Cove villagers for the desertion of Nai Tong Kok village. A more credible reason given was the almost total devastation during a 1937 typhoon, but a multitude of other interpretations were offered: the propensity of ghosts and devils for the place, the nearness of the sea, etc.

NOTES ON METHODOLOGY

Given the situation and the constraints under which this research project was to be conducted, the choice of a participant-observer methodology seemed the most rational.[1] The primary methodological problem was language. It had become obvious during an earlier study by one of the present authors that only native Hakka speakers could collect the kind of data in which we were interested — data concerning relatively private matters of family religious practice and individual religious belief.[2] Because of the lack of trained Hakka speaking social scientists in Hong Kong, this consideration limited us to a methodology which could be applied in the field by inexperienced observers.

In searching for observers we had several considerations in mind: the observer had to be willing to live in the resettlement area during the three-month period of field work;[3] at least one observer had to be a woman; all observers needed to be able to communicate at least crudely in English (so as to be able to converse with the authors) and fluently in Hakka. Using these criteria, we hired three observers, one a Hong Kong resident and the other two students from the Hakka speaking community in Sabah attending school in Hong Kong. The local person is a graduate of the Chinese University of Hong Kong and the other two are students in that institution. All were chosen on the basis of their interest in the project and their willingness to participate throughout the summer while living in the resettlement area.[4]

---

1 These considerations are reported in Morris I. Berkowitz, Frederick P. Brandauer and John H. Reed, "Study Program on Chinese Religious Practices in Hong Kong—A Progress Report," *Ching Feng*, XI, 3, 5-19, pp. 7-10.

2 See footnote 2 in the preface.

3 The main factors affecting the duration of time in the field were the personnel available as observers, all of whom were free only for the summer, and limited funds with which to finance their services. We realize that three months is a relatively short period of field work for this particular methodological approach. In order to minimize the effects of this short period of field work we sent observers periodically and on special occasions to supplement the data which had already been gathered.

4 We are grateful to the Sociology Department of Chung Chi College, the Chinese University of Hong Kong, for making available to us, gratis, living and working accommodations for our field workers.

Before moving the observers into the resettlement area, we gave them some preliminary training consisting of exposure to other social-scientific studies of Chinese villages, required reading and interpretation of a textbook on the fundamentals of social science methodology,[5] and practice observations in both contrived and field situations. Following the preliminary instruction, the observers moved to the apartment in Tai Po Market. They were instructed to begin their work by simply observing and describing what was happening around them without attempting to interview or otherwise intrude upon the lives of the villagers. The first task was to become recognized as residents of the resettlement area and to begin to establish friendships with some of the people living there.

Some readers may be surprised that three completely unrelated people, two men and a woman, could live in the same apartment without creating scandal, but dwelling space is so scarce in Hong Kong that relatively small dwelling places are often partitioned and shared by unrelated individuals of both sexes. Later in the summer the observers were joined by two Western women, one an anthropologist from the United States who was revisiting the villagers whom she had studied previously and the other a tutor in the Department of Sociology and Social Work of Chung Chi College. Other students doing field work also occasionally stayed for short periods. The apartment was undoubtedly a source of amusement, but not of concern, for the neighbours.

During this early period of observation, intensive training of the observers continued: periodically they came to meetings with Dr. Berkowitz and Mr. Reed at which their reports were reviewed, their problems discussed and new instructions issued. At these meetings, emphasis was placed on analysis of what the observer had done, for what he should have looked and what further data about the situations observed would have been more useful and would have made the reports more accurate. Throughout, the need for accuracy, detailed information and immediate recording of observations were stressed. In order not to hamper the observers with language difficulties, we permitted, indeed we insisted, that they write all of their reports in Chinese. Their field reports were later translated into English under the direction of Mr. Brandauer.

---

5 C. Selltiz, *et al.*, *Research Methods in Social Relations* (New York: Holt, Rinehart, Winston, 1962).

In this initial period we were attempting to describe the life situation and behaviour of the people of the resettlement area in as much detail as possible. At the outset, observation in public places seemed to provide the most useful training situations. These observations also had descriptive value as data for the project. Furthermore, the likelihood of gross errors was not as great, and we hoped to correct errors and add data by continually sending the observers back to the same situations. This insistence on obtaining a total picture of the life of the resettlement area results from the theoretical considerations already discussed in this volume.[6]

During this time the field workers were instructed to try to live as much as possible within the confines of the resettlement area—that is, they were asked to shop in the stores, eat in the restaurants, walk the streets. Extra money was provided them for the expense of trips to tea-houses and small stores which sold cold drinks and where people would congregate, and for other costs related to working in appropriate observational situations. Further, the observers were instructed to extend their observations around the clock and to avoid being consistently absent from the resettlement area at a given time of the week. During the first month of residence they were routinely responsible for the following situations: (1) each morning our female observer was to walk to the local bazaar to purchase her day's food, going at those times in the morning when the village women went (after a short time she never went without the company of some village housewives); (2) each observer was responsible for eating one meal at least three times a week at a local tea-house or restaurant and to begin to try to converse with the villagers in these situations;[7] and (3) the observers were instructed to meet and play with village children as frequently as possible in order that the children might eventually introduce the observers to their parents. On days when religious activities might occur, the observers had additional instructions concerning where to position themselves and for what phenomena to look.

The progress of the observers and the project during the first month was surprisingly rapid. The quality of the reports improved markedly, the amount of information which the observers produced

---

6 See Chapter I above.

7 The exception to this was our female observer whose frequent presence in the tea shops would almost surely have been frowned upon or at least noted as unusual.

was greater than expected and their success in integrating themselves into the community and becoming familiar with a large number of people was encouraging.

During the second month the observers were allowed considerable freedom to begin discussions with the resettled villagers, although they were still instructed not to breach the subject of religion. However, they had begun to make so many friends that had we limited their freedom to be as frank as the villagers expected, their behaviour might have been considered abnormal. The observers were instructed not to distort the reason for their presence when asked why they were there. They were advised to answer such queries by saying that they were Hakka people living in the resettlement area for their vacation and interested in the habits and customs of other Hakka people.

So far as we could determine, the villagers were neither offended nor much concerned by the presence of the observers. The people seemed to accept them as young persons who behaved "properly" according to Hakka tradition and therefore could be treated with the respect and consideration due to all Hakka people who do not violate fundamental behavioural expectations. Many of the people welcomed them because they provided new areas of conversation and could tell them about things in which they were interested: many of the villagers had relatives who had migrated to Sabah and therefore they were interested in the Chinese population there. In addition, some of the villagers took the opportunity to ask the observers to run errands for them and do other little chores, taking advantage of their literacy and their skills in the English language. They were asked to pay water bills, go to the District Office and run other errands which many of the villagers were reluctant to attempt. The observers offered their assistance willingly and as a result found themselves frequently treated to special favours: holiday foods, invitations to dinner and opportunities to drink tea in the afternoon were numerous. As often happens in field studies, some respondents tried to become observers by offering far more information than their own personal experience afforded them. The observers were constantly warned that these special efforts should be recorded like any other data, but should not be relied upon as totally accurate sources of information. That many of these volunteer informants reported inaccurately became apparent as the project developed.

During the final month and a half of observation, the observers were instructed to begin cautious semi-structured interviews with as broad a range of respondents as they had been able to make friends. Their fundamental instruction was to use a calendar of yearly events in Chinese religion as a series of prods in order to ask respondents what their religious practices during these events were.[8] In addition to "going around the calendar," as we came to call it, the observers were instructed to ask about practices on the first and fifteenth days of the lunar month and several other religious activities including ancestor worship. They were instructed not to be forward in interviewing. They were not to force a respondent to continue a discussion against his will but to finish the programme of questioning over a series of interviews. Several of the interviews continued for three or more sessions.

A primary concern was to make sure our observers did not get into difficult situations beyond their limited interviewing skills. We wanted them to have friendly talks rather than formal interviews. Thus, the normal rules of conversation were deemed to apply as opposed to the rules of formal interviews: when a respondent wished to change the subject, the interviewer was not to try to restrain him; when a respondent showed sensitivity and unwillingness to discuss an issue, the interviewer was to let it drop; when the respondent began to be bored and restless or uninterested, the interviewer was to cut off the interview and return and try again at a later time. The maintenance of the villagers' good will was considered more important than forced attempts to obtain answers to every possible question about every subject.

To summarize, we were concerned throughout with three different kinds of information: (1) we had, prior to our observers going into place, the results of the survey conducted by Berkowitz and associates; (2) we wanted consistent observational data about activities within the resettlement area including, but not limited to, religious activities; and (3) we wanted the results of semi-structured interviews directly concerned with religious practices.

We have noted that observers' reports were written in Chinese. After translation the reports were classified and filed according to content. The considerations involved in the classification scheme are reported elsewhere.[9] A simplified version of the scheme is reported on the following page.

---

8 See Chapter III for the significance of the calendar in Chinese religious observance.

9 Morris I. Berkowitz, *et al.,* "Study Program . . . , pp. 12-16.

OUTLINE OF CLASSIFICATION SCHEME

I. Life Style

    A. Dress
    B. Children's and Young People's Games and Activities
    C. Restaurant and Tea House Activity
    D. Social Activities
    E. Housekeeping Activity
    F. The Household
    G. Urbanization
    H. Conflict in the Resettlement Area

II. Family and Kinship

    A. General Structure
    B. Specific Family Structures
    C. Marriage
    D. Courtship

III. Social Structures
IV. Social Stratification
V. Economic Structure

    A. Fishing
    B. Farming
    C. Shopkeeping and Marketing
    D. Rentals
    E. Employment
    F. Money from England
    G. Obtaining Money to Use for Capital
    H. Ownership of Flats

VI. Education

    A. Primary School
    B. Secondary School
    C. Attitudes toward Schools

VII. Law

    A. British Laws Affecting Residents
    B. Enforcement of Laws
    C. Immigration

VIII. Religion

    A. Temples
    B. Religious Objects in the Home
    C. Religious Practice
    D. Religious Knowledge
    E. Conversation about Religion
    F. Attitudes about and Perceptions of Religion
    G. Gods, Spirits, Ghosts, etc.

IX. Population

    A. Individual Case Studies
    B. Health and Health Practices
    C. Old Age

X. History

    A. Villages
    B. Resettlement Area

BIBLIOGRAPHY OF WORKS CITED

Addison, J. T. *Chinese Ancestor Worship.* Shanghai: Church Literature Committee of the Chung Hua Sheng Kung Hui, 1925.

Aijmer, Goran. "Being Caught by a Fishnet: On Fengshui in Southeastern China," *Journal of the Hong Kong Branch of the Royal Asiatic Society,* VIII (1968), 75.

"Bai Qi Jie Qing Kuang Leng Dan" 拜七姐情況冷淡, *Wah Kiu Yat Po* 華僑日報, July 31, 1968.

Baker, Hugh D. R. *Sheung Shui, A Chinese Lineage Village.* London: Frank Cass, 1968.

Barnett, K. M. A. "The People of the New Territories" in *Hong Kong Business Symposium, A Compilation of Authoritative Views on the Administration, Commerce and Resources of Britain's Far Eastern Outpost.* comp. J. M. Braga. Hong Kong: South China Morning Post, 1957.

Bavelas, Alex. "Communication Patterns in Task-Oriented Groups," *Journal of the Acoustical Society of America,* 22 (1950), 725-730.

Becker, Howard. *Modern Sociological Theory in Continuity and Change.* New York: Holt, Rinehart and Winston, 1957.

Becker, Howard and H. E. Barnes. *Social Thought from Lore to Science.* New York: Dover Publications, 1961.

Berkowitz, Morris I. "Ecology and Human Behavior: A Comparison of Rural and Urban Environments and Their Effects on Resettled Hakka Villagers" in *Conservation and Development of the Countryside* (tentative title). ed. J. A. Prescott. Hong Kong: Hong Kong University Press, 1970.

Berkowitz, Morris I. "Plover Cove Village to Tai Po Market: A Study in Forced Migration," *Journal of the Hong Kong Branch of the Royal Asiatic Society,* VIII (August, 1968), 96-108.

Berkowitz, M. I., F. P. Brandauer and J. H. Reed. "Study Program on Chinese Religious Practices in Hong Kong — A Progress Report," *Ching Feng*, XI (1968), 3, 5-19.

Boyd, Andrew. *Chinese Architecture and Town Planning.* London: Alec Tiranti, 1962.

Bracey, D. H. "The Effects of Emigration on a Hakka Village" (unpubl. diss.). Cambridge, Massachusetts: Harvard University Library, 1967.

Bunzel, Ruth. "The Economic Organization of Primitive People" in *General Anthropology.* ed. Franz Boas. New York: Johnson Reprint Corporation, 1965.

Burkhardt, V. R. *Chinese Creeds and Customs.* 3 vols. Hong Kong: South China Morning Post, 1955.

Caillois, Roger. *Man and the Sacred.* trans. Meyer Barash. Glencoe, Illinois: Free Press, 1959.

Campisi, Paul J. "The Italian Family in the United States" in *Selected Studies in Marriage and the Family.* ed. Robert F. Winch, Robert McGinnis and Herbert R. Barringer. New York: Holt, Rinehart and Winston, 1962.

Cao Yu 曹楡 . "Qi Qiao Jie Za Tan" 乞巧節雜談, *Sing Tao Jih Pao* 星島日報, August 1, 1968.

Chen Ta. *Emigrant Communities in South China: A Study of Overseas Migration and Its Influences on Standards of Living and Social Change.* New York: Institute of Pacific Relations, 1940.

Couling, Samuel. *Encyclopaedia Sinica.* Shanghai: Kelly and Walsh, 1917.

Crook, David and Isabel Crook. *Revolution in a Chinese Village: Ten Mile Inn.* London: Routledge, Kegan Paul, 1959.

De Groot, J. J. M. *The Religion of the Chinese.* New York: MacMillan, 1912.

De Groot, J. J. M. *The Religious System of China.* Taipei: Ch'eng Wen, 1967.

Dennys, N. B. *The Folk-Lore of China.* London: Trübner, 1876.

de Rohan Barondes, R. *China: Lore, Legend and Lyrics.* London: Peter Owen, 1959.

Doré, Henry. *Researches into Chinese Superstitions.* Taipei: Ch'eng Wen, 1966.

Durkheim, Emile. "On Communal Ritual" in *Theories of Society.* trans. Joseph W. Swain (1954). ed. Talcott Parsons, *et. al.* Glencoe, Illinois: Free Press, 1961.

Eberhard, Wolfram. *Chinese Festivals.* New York: Henry Shuman, 1952.

Eliade, Mircea. *The Sacred and the Profane, The Nature of Religion.* trans. Willard R. Trask. New York: Harper & Row, 1961.

The Encyclopedic Dictionary of the Chinese Language 中文大辭典. Taipei: The Institute for Advanced Chinese Studies, 1968.

Fei Hsiao Tung. *Peasant Life in China.* London: Routledge & Kegan Paul, 1939.

Fenn, C. H. *The Five Thousand Dictionary.* Peking: College of Chinese Studies, 1940.

Festinger, L. "Architecture and Group Membership," *Journal of Social Issues,* 7 (1951), 152-163.

Festinger, L. and H. H. Kelley. *Changing Attitudes Through Social Contact.* Ann Arbor, Michigan: Research Center for Group Dynamics, 1951.

Fitzgerald, C. P. *China.* 3rd ed. London: Cresset Press, 1961.

Franke, Wolfgang. "The Taiping Rebellion" in *The China Reader,* Vol. 1: *Imperial China.* trans. Franz Schurmann. ed. Franz Schurmann and Orville Schell. New York: Vintage Books, 1967.

Freedman, Maurice. "Ancestor Worship: Two Facets of the Chinese Case" in *Social Organization: Essays Presented to Raymond Firth.* ed. Maurice Freedman. London: Frank Cass, 1967.

Freedman, Maurice. *Chinese Lineage and Society: Fukien and Kwangtung.* University of London: Athlone Press, 1966.

Friedrich, Paul. "Semantic Structure and Social Structure: An Instance from Russian" in *Explorations in Cultural Anthropology*. ed. Ward H. Goodenough. New York: McGraw Hill, 1964.

Gallin, Bernard. *Hsin Hsing, Taiwan: A Chinese Village in Change*. Berkeley: University of California Press, 1966.

A Gazetteer of Place Names in Hong Kong, Kowloon and the New Territories. Hong Kong: Hong Kong Government Press, 1960.

Giles, Herbert. *A Chinese-English Dictionary*. Taipei: Ch'eng Wen, 1967.

Goode, William J. "A Theory of Role Strain" in *Selected Studies in Marriage and the Family*. ed. Robert F. Winch, Robert McGinnis and Herbert R. Barringer. New York: Holt, Rinehart and Winston, 1963.

Goode, William J. *Religion Among the Primitives*. Glencoe, Illinois: Free Press, 1951.

Graham, David Crockett. *Folk Religion in Southwest China*. Washington, D.C.: Smithsonian Press, 1961.

Granet, Marcel. *La Religion des Chinois*. Paris: Presses Universitaires de France, 1957.

Groves, Robert G. "The Origins of Two Market Towns in the New Territories" in *Aspects of Social Organization in the New Territories*. ed. M. Topley. Hong Kong: The Hong Kong Branch of the Royal Asiatic Society, 1964.

Handlin, Oscar. *The Uprooted*. Boston: Little Brown, 1951.

Hayes, James W. "Geomancy and the Village" in *Some Traditional Chinese Ideas and Conceptions in Hong Kong Social Life Today*. ed. Marjorie Topley. Hong Kong: The Hong Kong Branch of the Royal Asiatic Society, 1966.

Hayes, James W. "The Japanese Occupation and the New Territories," *The South China Morning Post,* December 15, 1967.

Hayes, James W. "Movement of Villages on Lantau Island for Fung Shui Reasons," *Journal of the Hong Kong Branch of the Royal Asiatic Society,* III (1963), 43-44.

Hayes, James W. "The Pattern of Life in the New Territories in 1898," *Journal of the Hong Kong Branch of the Royal Asiatic Society,* II (1962), 75-102.

Huang P. F., Parker. *Speak Cantonese.* 3 vols. New Haven, Connecticut: Far Eastern Publications, Yale University, 1962.

James, William. *The Varieties of Religious Experience.* New York: New American Library, 1958.

Jin Ling 金鈴. "Wo Guo De Qing Ren Jie" 我國的情人節, *Wah Kiu Yat Po* 華僑日報, July 30, 1968.

Krone, The Rev. Mr. "A Notice of the Sanon District," *Journal of the Hong Kong Branch of the Royal Asiatic Society,* VII (1967), 104-137.

Langer, Susanne K. *Philosophy in a New Key.* Cambridge, Massachusetts: Harvard University Press, 1957.

Latourette, Kenneth Scott. *The Chinese: Their History and Culture.* New York: MacMillan, 1964.

Lechler, R. "The Hakka Chinese," *The Chinese Recorder,* 9 (1878), 352-359.

Lewin, Kurt. "Behavior and Development as a Function of the Total Situation" in *Manual of Child Psychology.* ed. L. Carmichael. New York: Wiley, 1946.

Lewis, Oscar. *Tepoztlán: Villagers in Mexico.* New York: Holt, Rinehart and Winston, 1965.

Linton, Ralph. *The Study of Man.* New York: Appleton-Century Crofts, 1963.

Liu Wu Chi. *An Introduction to Chinese Literature.* Bloomington: Indiana University Press, 1966.

Lo Hsiang-lin 羅香林. *Historical Sources for the Study of the Hakkas* 客家史料滙編. Hong Kong: Institute of Chinese Culture, 1965.

Lo Hsiang-lin, *et al. Hong Kong and Its External Communications Before 1842, The History of Hong Kong Prior to British Arrival.* Hong Kong: Institute of Chinese Culture, 1963.

Malinowski, Bronislaw. *Magic, Science and Religion.* New York: Doubleday Anchor Books, 1948.

March, Andrew L. "An Appreciation of Chinese Geomancy," *Journal of Asian Studies,* XXVII: 2 (February, 1968), 259.

Matthews, R. H. *Chinese-English Dictionary.* Cambridge, Massachusetts: Harvard University Press, 1945.

Mead, George H. *Mind, Self, and Society.* ed. C. W. Morris. Chicago: University of Chicago Press, 1934.

Merton, Robert K. *Social Theory and Social Structure.* New York: Free Press, 1957.

Needham, Joseph. *Science and Civilization in China.* Cambridge, Massachusetts: Harvard University Press, 1956.

The New Golden Bough. ed. James G. Frazer and Theodor H. Gastor. New York: Criterion Books, 1959.

Newcomb, Theodore. *Social Psychology.* New York: Dryden Press, 1950.

O'Dea, Thomas F. *The Sociology of Religion.* Englewood Cliffs, New Jersey: Prentice-Hall, 1966.

Oehler, W. "Christian Work Among the Hakkas" in *The Christian Occupation of China.* ed. M. T. Stauffer. Shanghai: China Continuation Committee, 1922.

Papers Laid Before the Legislative Council of Hong Kong, 1911. Hong Kong: Hong Kong Government Press.

Park, Robert E. *Race and Culture.* Glencoe, Illinois: Free Press, 1950.

Parsons, Talcott. *The Structure of Social Action.* 2nd ed. Glencoe, Illinois: Free Press, 1949.

Pratt, J. A. "Emigration and Unilineal Descent Groups, A Study of Marriage in a Hakka Village in the New Territories, Hong Kong," *The Eastern Anthropologist,* XIII, 4 (June-August, 1960), 147-149.

"Qi Qiao Jie Ming Jie Lin Bai Xian Zhi Feng Da Jian" 乞巧節明屆臨拜仙之風大減, *Wah Kiu Yat Po* 華僑日報, July 29, 1968.

"Qi Xi Yu Lan Jian Jin Mang Sha Zha Zuo Gong Ren" 七夕盂蘭漸近忙煞紮作工人, *Wah Kiu Yat Po* 華僑日報, July 26, 1968.

Redfield, Robert. *Peasant Society and Culture*. Chicago: University of Chicago Press, 1956.

Reichelt, K. L. *Religion in Chinese Garment*. London: Lutterworth Press, 1951.

Selltiz, C., *et. al. Research Methods in Social Relations*. New York: Holt, Rinehart and Winston, 1962.

Skinner, G. W. "Marketing and Social Structure in Rural China," *Journal of Asian Studies*, XXIV, 1,2,3 (1964-1965).

Smith, D. Howard. *Chinese Religions*. London: Weidenfeld and Nicolson, 1968.

Soothill, W. E. *The Three Religions of China*. 3rd ed. London: Oxford University Press, 1930.

Sources of Chinese Tradition. ed. Wm. Theodore de Bary. New York: Columbia University Press, 1966.

Thomas, William I. and Florian Znaniecki. *The Polish Peasant in Europe and America*. Boston: Gorham Press, 1918.

Tönnies, Ferdinand. *Community and Society (Gemeinschaft und Gesellschaft)*. trans. Charles P. Loomis. East Lansing: Michigan State University Press, 1957.

Tsang, O. Z. 張雲鵬編. *A New Complete Chinese-English Dictionary* 最新漢英大辭典. Hong Kong: Great China Book Company, 1966.

Veblen, T. *Theory of the Leisure Class*. New York: Modern Library, 1934.

Wach, Joachim. *Sociology of Religion*. Chicago: University of Chicago Press, 1944.

Wach, Joachim. *Types of Religious Experience, Christian and Non-Christian*. Chicago: University of Chicago Press, 1952.

Weber, Max. *Ancient Judaism.* trans. & ed. H. H. Gerth and D. Martindale. Glencoe, Illinois: Free Press, 1952.

Weber, Max. "Religious Rejections of the World and Their Directions" in *From Max Weber.* trans. H. H. Gerth and C. Wright Mills. Galaxy Book ed. New York, 1958.

Weber, Max. *The Protestant Ethic and the Spirit of Capitalism.* trans. Talcott Parsons. New York: Charles Scribner's Sons, 1958.

Weber, Max. *The Religion of China: Confucianism and Taoism.* trans. H. H. Gerth. New York: MacMillian, 1964.

Weber, Max. *The Sociology of Religion.* Boston: Beacon Press, 1963.

Werner, E. T. C. *A Dictionary of Chinese Mythology.* New York: Julian Press, 1961.

Werner, E. T. C. *Myths and Legends of China.* London: George G. Harrap, 1922.

Whyte, William F. *Street Corner Society.* Chicago: University of Chicago Press, 1960.

Williams, C. A. S. *Encyclopedia of Chinese Symbolism and Art Motives.* New York: Julian Press, 1960.

Wirth, Louis. *On Cities and Social Life.* ed. A. J. Reiss, Jr. Chicago: University of Chicago Press, 1964.

Xu Ma Shu Sheng 戎馬書生. "Nian Nian Qi Yu Ren Jian Qiao" 年年乞與人間巧, *Sing Tao Man Pao* 星島晚報, August 1, 1968.

Xue Sheng Xiao Zi Dian 學生小字典. Hong Kong: Commercial Press. 1952.

Yang, C. K. *Religion in Chinese Society.* Berkeley: University of California Press, 1967.

Yang, C. K. "The Functional Relation Between Confucian Thought and Chinese Religion" in *Chinese Thought and Institutions.* ed. John K. Fairbank. Chicago: University of Chicago Press, 1957.

Yang, Martin C. *A Chinese Village.* London: Kegan Paul, Trench, Trübner, 1948.

Yinger, J. Milton. *Religion, Society and the Individual.* New York: MacMillian, 1957.

GLOSSARY

The romanizations used in the text are listed alphabetically in the left-hand column. The Pinyin Latinization[1] has been used except for officially recognized romanizations of proper names.[2] Also included is a third column giving the Yale Cantonese Romanization for the terms in Pinyin.[3]

Bai nian	拜年	Baai nihn
Bai Qi Jie Qing Kuang Leng Dan	拜七姐情況冷淡	Baai Chat Jeh Chihng Fong Laahng Daahm
Bao Ri	報日	Bou Yaht
Ben di	本地	Bun deih
Bo Gong	伯公	Baak Gung
Bo Po	伯婆	Baak Poh
Cai	蔡	Choi
Canton	廣州	
Cao Yu	曹楡	Chouh Yuh
Chong Yang	重陽	Chuhng Yeuhng
Chu	楚	Cho
Chun Qiu Zuo Zhuan	春秋左傳	Cheun Chau Jo Jyuhn
Chung Mei	涌尾	
Chung Pui	涌背	
Ci tang	祠堂	Chih tohng
Da Wang	大王	Daaih Wohng
Da Wang Ye	大王爺	Daaih Wohng Yeh
Di	帝	Dai
Di Zhu Shen	地主神	Deih Jyu Sahn
Fanling	粉嶺	

---

[1] *Xue Sheng Xiao Zi Dian* 學生小字典 (Hong Kong: Commercial Press, 1952).

[2] *A Gazetteer of Place Names in Hong Kong, Kowloon and the New Territories* (Hong Kong: Hong Kong Government Press, 1960).

[3] Parker P. F. Huang, *Speak Cantonese, Books I-III* (New Haven: Far Eastern Publications, Yale University, 1962).

Feng shui	風水	Fung seui
Feng shui xian sheng	風水先生	Fung seui sin saang
Fu	符	Fuh
Fu De Hui	福德會	Fuk Dak Wuih
Fukien	福建	
Gong de	功德	Gung dak
Gong xi fa cai, li shi dou lai	恭喜發財，利是掹來	Gung hei faat choih, leih sih dauh loih
Guan Di	關帝	Gwaan Dai
Guan Fu Zi	關夫子	Gwaan Fu Ji
Guan Gong	關公	Gwaan Gung
Guan Shi Yin	觀世音	Gun Sai Yam
Guan Yin	觀音	Gun Yam
Guan Yu	關羽	Gwaan Yuh
Gui	鬼	Gwai
Hakka	客家	
Han	漢	Hon
Hao ming po	好命婆	Hou mihng poh
Hong Kong	香港	
Hua dai	花帶	Fa daai
Hun	魂	Wahn
Hun shu	婚書	Fan syu
Jie Zhi Tui	介之推	Gaai Ji Teui
Jin	斤	Gan
Jin Ling	金鈴	Gam Lihng
Jin ta	金塔	Gam taap
Jin ta ci	金塔祠	Gam taap chih
Kai Guang	開光	Hoi Gwong
Kai jian	開剪	Hoi jin
Kai mian	開面	Hoi mihn
Kam Chuk Pai	金竹排	
Kang Xi	康熙	Hong Hei
Kiangsi	江西	
Kong Ming	孔明	Hung Mihng
Kowloon	九龍	
Kwangtung	廣東	

Kwong Fuk	廣福	
Lei	李	
Li	里	Leih
Li shi	利市，利是	Leih sih
Li tou	犁頭	Laih tauh
Lin	林	Lahm
Liu Bei	劉備	Lauh Beih
Liu li	六禮	Luhk laih
Lu Ye Shui	綠葉水	Luhk Yihp Seui
Luo ge	羅格	Loh gaak
Ma Niang	媽娘	Ma Neuhng
Ma Po	麻婆	Mah Poh
Man yue	滿月	Muhn yuht
Men Kou Tu Di Fu Shen	門口土地福神	Muhn Hau Tou Deih Fuk Sahn
Mi Luo	汨羅	Mihk Loh
Miao Shan	妙善	Miuh Sihn
Ming	明	Mihng
Na cai	納采	Naahp choi
Na ji	納吉	Naahp gat
Nai Tong Kok	泥塘角	
Nian Nian Qi Yu Ren Jian Qiao	年年乞與人間巧	Nihn Nihn Hat Yuh Yahn Gaan Haau
Niu Lang	牛郎	Ngauh Lohng
Nuo mi	糯米	Noh maih
Pat Sin	八仙	
Pin shu	聘書	Ping Syu
Po	魄	Paak
Pun Chung	泮涌	
Qi	戚	Chik
Qi lin	麒麟	Keih leuhn
Qi po	七魄	Chat paak
Qi Qiao Jie	乞巧節	Hat Haau Jit
Qi Qiao Jie Ming Jie Lin Bai Xian Zhi Feng Da Jian	乞巧節明屆臨拜仙之風大減	Hat Haau Jit Mihng Gaai Lahm Baai Sin Ji Fung Daaih Gaam

Qi Qiao Jie Za Tan	乞巧節雜談	Hat Haau Jit Jaahp Taahm
Qi Xi Yu Lan Jian Jin Mang Sha Zha Zuo Gong Ren	七夕盂蘭漸近 忙煞紮作工人	Chat Jihk Yuh Laahn Jihm Gahn Mohng Saat Jaat Johk Gung Yahn
Qi Yue	七約	Chat Yeuk
Qin	秦	Cheuhn
Qin ying	親迎	Chan yihng
Qing Ming	清明	Ching Mihng
Qing qi	請期	Cheng keih
Qu Yuan	屈原	Wat Yuhn
Saam Gwong	三光	
San Guo Zhi Yan Yi	三國志演義	Saam Gwok Ji Yin Yih
San hun	三魂	Saam wahn
San jiao wei yi	三教爲一	Saam gaau waih yat
San shu	三書	Saam syu
Sha Tau Kok	沙頭角	
Shan ku	衫褲	Saam fu
Shang	商	Seung
Shansi	山西	
Shen	神	Sahn
Shen jia yin	身嫁銀	San ga ngahn
Sing Tao Jih Pao	星島日報	
Sing Tao Man Pao	星島晚報	
Siu Kau	小滘	
Sun Quan	孫權	Syun Kyuhn
Tai Kau	大滘	
Tai Lung	大龍	
Tai Mei Tuk	大美篤	
Tai Po	大埔	
Tai Zong	太宗	Taai Jung
Taiping	太平	
Tang	唐	Tohng
Tian Guan Ci Fu	天官賜福	Tin Gun Chi Fuk
Tian Hou	天后	Tin Hauh

Tu Di	土地	Tou Deih
Tu Di Shen	土地神	Tou Deih Sahn
Tung Sau	同壽	
Wah Kiu Yat Po	華僑日報	
Wan	溫	
Wang Leng Tau	橫嶺頭	
Wen ming	問名	Mahn meng
Wo Guo De Qing Ren Jie	我國的情人節	Ngoh Gwok Dik Chihng Yahn Jit
Wong	王	
Wu	武	Mouh
Wu Kau Tang	烏蛟騰	
Wu Po	巫婆	Mouh Poh
Wu San Kuei	吳三桂	
Wu Yue Jie	五月節	Ng Yuht Jit
Xi	喜	Hei
Xiao xiang gun	孝相棍	Haau seung gwan
Xu Ma Shu Sheng	戎馬書生	Seut Mah Syu Saang
Xuan Zong	玄宗	Yuhn Jung
Yan	雁	Ngahn
Yang	陽	Yeuhng
Yang Gui Fei	楊貴妃	Yeuhng Gwai Fei
Yao	堯	Yiuh
Yin	陰	Yam
Yin ding	銀錠	Ngahn ding
Yip	葉	
You zi	柚子	Yauh ji
Yuan bao ding	元寶錠	Yuhn bou ding
Yue	越	Yuht
Yuen Long	元朗	
Yuk Kwan	育群	
Yun shu	允書	Wahn syu
Zao	灶	Jou
Zao Jun Shen	灶君神	Jou Gwan Sahn
Zhang	張	Jeung
Zhang Fei	張飛	Jeung Fei

Zheng Cheng Gong	鄭成功	Jehng Sihng Gung
Zhi Nü	織女	Jik Neuih
Zhi Shu Jie	植樹節	Jihk Syuh Jit
Zhou	周	Jau
Zi you lian ai	自由戀愛	Jih yauh lyuhn oi
Zong	粽	Jung
Zu bu	族布	Juhk bou
Zuo Zhuan	左傳	Jo Jyuhn

INDEX